YOUR PERFECT BODY

A STATE OF MIND

Geoff Slattery Publishing Pty Ltd
140 Harbour Esplanade, Docklands, Vic. 3008
www.geoffslattery.com.au

First published 2004

National Library of Australia
Cataloguing-in-Publication data

Harper, Craig, 1963- .
Your perfect body : a state of mind : the business of you.

ISBN 0 9752255 5 3.

1. Attitude change. 2. Physical fitness. 3. Health. I. Title.

613.7

Cover and page design by Paul Marcolin
Managing editor: Geoff Slattery
Illustrations by Guy Shield

Printed by Griffin Press

THE BUSINESS OF YOU

YOUR PERFECT BODY

A STATE OF MIND

CRAIG HARPER

gspbooks

CONTENTS

Foreword The business of you 7

Introduction New attitude, new behaviours, new body 8

Section One AN APPRAISAL OF YOU

Chapter 1 **Your perfect body** 16

Chapter 2 **Jumbo** 23

Chapter 3 **Question your beliefs** 30

Chapter 4 **It's all about attitude** 37

Chapter 5 **Motivation and inspiration** 43

Section Two LET'S GET STARTED

Chapter 6 **A business plan – for your body** 52

Chapter 7 **The preliminaries** 56

Chapter 8 **Action starts here** 65

Chapter 9 **How to eat well** 74

Chapter 10 **How to exercise well** 99

Section Three COMMON FAILINGS AND HOW TO BEAT THEM

Chapter 11 **Falling off the wagon** 110

Chapter 12 **Finish what you start** 113

Chapter 13 **The time factor** 120

Chapter 14 **The fine line between discipline and obsession** 126

Chapter 15 **It's about you, not your 'mates'** 130

Chapter 16 **Social eating** 134

Chapter 17 **Don't confuse the six-pack with inner peace** 139

Chapter 18 **Don't be a spoilsport** 141

Section Four **CASE STUDIES**

Chapter 19 **Jan & Ian: older bodies, younger attitude** 146

Chapter 20 **'Maggie': a turn for the better** 151

Chapter 21 **Craig: the sick obsessive** 154

Chapter 22 **'Bill': finding the right program for you** 157

Chapter 23 **Jim Solopitias** 159

Chapter 24 **Artie Kalnins** 161

Chapter 25 **Captain inconsistency** 163

Chapter 26 **'George': too much training, too little recovery** .. 165

Section Five **A PERSONAL ACCOUNT**

Chapter 27 **Marlo** 168

Section Six **AND FINALLY ...**

Epilogue **Are you ready to change forever?** 180

Appendix **Example of a food and training diary entry** 186

The Business of You

This is the second in the series titled The Business of You, and follows what appears to be a very different book called *The Book of Success (volume one)*. That is a book of interviews with people from all walks of life who have applied a mix of business skills, common sense, and never-say-die attitude to their dream.

Your Perfect Body, a State of Mind is based on exactly the same premise: business practice, common sense and a never-say-die attitude are the basis of Craig Harper's philosophy of getting fit, and staying fit. Like all businesses, an assessment is required, a plan developed, and that plan applied to achieve the goal.

In this case the business is absolutely YOU: it's your body, and the Harper approach is to give YOU the plan, and expect YOU to employ it. Like the CEO of any major company, he is giving his 'employee' (you) the right resources to do the business expected: it's up to you to accept that freedom, be excited by its potential, and make sure the outcome is just what you – and he – expected.

Series Editor

Geoff Slattery

NEW ATTITUDE, NEW BEHAVIOURS, NEW BODY

I regularly talk to people who have been overweight and out of shape for most of their life and invariably they will tell me with absolute certainty that they cannot lose weight. For some sad reason it seems that they have convinced themselves that the 'battle of the bulge' is their life-long destiny; a life of struggle, embarrassment and heartache.

Will not and cannot are two different things. If you've never created your ideal body, don't assume you can't; just assume you haven't yet. As I write this I am in better shape at 40 years of age than I was at 30 or even 20 and certainly 14!

That's not meant to happen. Most 'experts' would tell you that as you age you'll be getting fatter, weaker and less fit. Guess what? You don't need to.

I expect that when I am 50 years old I will be in the shape I'm in now, if not better; not because I am a genetic freak (quite the opposite), but because I know how incredibly adaptable the human body is when we stimulate it the right way and we get that incredible thing called our mind in the right place.

Why does a society which is consistently bombarded with more and more information about obesity and the associated diseases continue to overeat and under-exercise and why do people who hate being fat consistently embrace behaviours which lead to obesity?

In the quest for a better body some people go from expert to expert hoping to find the one who will tell them what they want to hear. They do this because they figure there 'must be an easier way.' Sometimes we need to stop looking for the 'easy' way and just do what works. When you stop looking for the easy way, you'll be astounded at how easily and how quickly you can change your physiology.

A common mistake made by the health and fitness professions is to approach the 'getting in shape' process from a purely 'physical' perspective; lift this, stretch those, run there, eat that.

'Okay, that's the program from a practical perspective, but what about my lack of motivation? What about my hatred for exercise? What about those five gym memberships I didn't use? What about those 300 diets I've started and stopped? What about my obsessive behaviour around food? What about my chocolate addiction? What about my crappy attitude?'

Creating your perfect body for life is not about choosing the 'best' program or diet, it's about arriving at a point emotionally and psychologically where you are genuinely ready to turn your life, your thinking and your body around.

By the way, when I use the term *perfect body* I am not talking about some stereotypical Hollywood creation with three per cent bodyfat, perfect proportions and surgically enhanced everything, I am talking about the best body for you based on your age, your genetics, the shape you're in right now and what it is you want to achieve.

For the purpose of this book I will use the term *perfect body* as a generic description for the changes you individually want to make to create *your perfect body*. 'Perfect' may mean smaller, bigger, leaner, more muscle, less muscle, lighter, faster, fitter, stronger, healthier and so on. Perfect means whatever it means to you – it may have nothing to do with appearance and everything to do with feeling great and functioning optimally. It is completely individual and personal.

Most people come to see me with pretty standard goals, such as 'I want to be leaner, lighter and I want more muscle definition' or 'I want to look like that guy from *Triple X* (Vin Diesel) or that girl from *Lara Croft Tomb Raider* (Angelina Jolie) by next Tuesday.' Not too many people visit me because they want to make the Olympic team.

People often have drastically different goals, depending on what they consider to be attractive and desirable. The truth is that most of us are more concerned with how we look than we are with how we function. About 90 per cent of the people that I talk to, want to be leaner – lean is the desired look at the moment. There is no 'ideal body' and what one person views as desirable or attractive will be to another, undesirable and repulsive.

If you have ever been to a bodybuilding competition and experienced the bodybuilding culture then you will understand that beauty is indeed in the eye of the beholder. I have several bodybuilders who work with me and I am always amused by the different reactions that the same body can generate. Gary, one of my trainers, has won several state titles and is one of the better competitive bodybuilders in Australia. On a daily basis his appearance will draw comments ranging from:

'that's disgusting' to
'that's gorgeous', and from
'I would never want to look like that' to
'how long will it take me to look like you?'

It is a good thing that he is not too precious or he would be in therapy for the next 10 years. We all have a different picture in our mind of what is an attractive and desirable form. For some people, the bigger the better, for others it is just the opposite.

In 20 years of trying to help people create their *perfect body*, I have learned that whether or not people achieve their goals sometimes *has very little to do with*:

1. The program they choose to follow.
2. The nutritional philosophy they embrace.
3. The equipment and resources they have at their disposal.
4. What they know.

Most times it has everything to do with the individual's ability to stay focused, deal with a little discomfort and finish what they start.

For years I have found it frustrating to see clients and friends reading book after book extolling the virtues of this diet, that new revolutionary piece of equipment or this new training philosophy, only to find that after a period of time the euphoria has subsided and that particular book, system or method has made way for the 'newer, better and quicker' approach.

In writing *this* book I want to challenge you and motivate you to take action (not for 10 minutes but for life) and to help you address old issues in new ways. To a certain extent we all create our own reality and we all make our endeavours harder or easier than the next person, depending on how we approach them. For years I have watched people create a life of misery for themselves because they consistently choose <u>not</u> to make decisions, not to be responsible, not to be proactive and not to have a good attitude.

Let's be clear about one thing: where we end up (and what state our body is in) is largely about choices not about fate, circumstances or genetics.

As a trainer I work with some people who achieve great results and some who don't, even though I provide everyone with the same opportunities. Why? Because ultimately success and failure always comes back to you, the individual; not what you read or hear or know but how you behave and what you do, over the course of time.

Keep in mind that while a book can be a valuable tool and a catalyst for change, it is just a bunch of pages with someone's ideas and thoughts on them – a book can't make the changes for you. Having a map in your hands won't get you to a destination, but following the map will.

How valuable this book or any resource will be to you, the reader, will depend on what you do with the information – it's not what you know; it's what you do with what you know.

In the following chapters I am going to talk to you exactly as I do to my clients. I will tell you the truth and I will give you the real deal on getting in shape and creating your perfect body. I am not renowned for candy-coating my message and I won't necessarily tell you what you want to hear, but I will be honest and I will tell you what genuinely works and what doesn't. There's even a section which lists most of the excuses I've heard, excuses for those who have failed, or almost failed. It's there for you when you find your endeavour is drifting. Don't worry, that happens to all of us. To balance that, I've included many case studies, examples of people who have faced down the challenge, and won out.

It is my hope that, for you, this book will be the catalyst for a different body, a different attitude, a different reality and an amazing future. If you are tired of going around in circles and living in a body that is less than your ideal, then I dare you to not only read, but DO and see what happens when you genuinely do EVERYTHING WITHIN YOUR POWER to create life-long change.

The one thing that everyone who buys a book such as this has in common is the desire to change. If you're reading this then I can safely assume that you're not completely happy with how you look or feel at this point in time. Creating genuine 'forever change' (a term you will become familiar with) is about being able to take the information I'm going to give you, adjusting your mind and lifestyle accordingly, creating a realistic and practical plan and getting on with it. It is as difficult as we – you – make it.

Anyone who succeeds in any endeavour has a plan, a method, some resources and an appropriate attitude – creating your perfect body is not a hit and miss process. Too many people live in a body they hate because they consistently fail to manage their greatest resource (their body) and consistently look for the fast, easy option. In this book I am going to tell you why some people fail and some succeed, why some make it easy and some make it an absolute misery, and finally, I will teach how and why your mind is the greatest and most under-estimated weight-loss tool available.

I am fortunate enough to have a job where I am constantly surrounded by ordinary people achieving amazing things, all of them following the principles I will outline. One of the qualities I admire in successful people is that they are prepared to question pre-existing beliefs, think outside the box and to look at old issues or events or experiences from a new perspective. They are also prepared to get uncomfortable on a regular basis; don't be scared to get uncomfortable or to stretch yourself.

Putting ourselves in challenging situations is how we learn, grow, acquire new skills and develop strength of character. Life is uncomfortable. If you don't get uncomfortable on a regular basis you're not learning or growing.

We all create our own reality; if we say it is going to be hard, it will be. Changing your body can be a challenging and uncomfortable process, but many of us make it harder than it needs to be. Changing your body can also be an absolutely life-changing and reality-changing experience, far beyond the physical.

Achieving your better body can help you:

- Cope more effectively with mental and emotional stress.
- Function better in the workplace.
- Live longer with a better quality of life.
- Have better relationships.
- Improve your sex life.
- See things from a more positive perspective.
- Be better role models for your family and friends.
- Boost confidence and self-esteem to be able to achieve in other areas of your life.
- Be a more pleasant person to be around.
- Drastically improve your energy levels.

So what are you waiting for? Resolve that from now you are going to do the things necessary to get you where you want to go.

Craig Harper
September 2004.

SECTION ONE

AN APPRAISAL OF YOU

The first thing you must do is work out who you are, what you want to achieve and how you intend to get there. You can do it, but you must commit and you must be honest with yourself.

Chapter 1	**Your perfect body** A case of mind and body	16
Chapter 2	**Jumbo** Craig Harper's teenage life change	23
Chapter 3	**Question your beliefs** Questions lead to positive change	30
Chapter 4	**It's all about attitude** Positive thoughts ... positive results	37
Chapter 5	**Motivation and inspiration** Be inspired, not motivated	43

CHAPTER 1

YOUR PERFECT BODY

To achieve your perfect body, you'll need to understand that physical change and psychological change go hand in hand.

In my job as a personal trainer and exercise scientist I rarely meet people who are completely happy with their body. In fact, many of the people I talk to tell me they 'hate' their body.

They want change. They want to be leaner, lighter, healthier, stronger, fitter, more energised or even sexier.

While some of us have had these aspirations to create some type of physical change for a very long time, many of us seem to be perpetually treading water and forever looking at that spare tyre, those chunky thighs or those love handles with disdain.

While most of us have the potential to shape up and change our body significantly, the reality is that most of us don't, or if we do, we don't stay in shape forever.

Many of us seem to alternate between in-shape and out-of-shape in an annual ritual of frustration. Alternating between fit and fat is not what we want. It is not good for our body or for our mind.

In Australia, right now we have more weight-loss and body-enhancement options than ever before.

If your goal is to shape up, then you have a multitude of choices and options as to how you might approach the *getting in shape* process.

The list looks something like this:

Gyms, personal trainers, dieticians, pills that stop your body from absorbing fat, pills that stop hunger, pills that shed water, pills that increase your metabolic rate, protein powders, bars that get you massive and ripped in no time, lite (whatever that means) meals, hypnotherapy, stomach stapling, liposuction, psychologists, obesity counsellors, seminars, books, specialised restaurants, health sanctuaries (fat farms), cereals that taste like flavoured sand (but have no fat or sugar!), the 'ab-blaster 4000' (only seven minutes a day) and let's not forget my personal favourite; the 'vibrating belt' that simply sits on your hips and melts away the fat while you relax.

Too easy.

It's obviously not. Look at the facts: we are better educated, better informed and better equipped to get in shape than ever before, but according to the Australian Bureau of Statistics the average Australian gets a little larger every year. In 1989-90, 36 per cent of people aged 15 and over were overweight or obese. This increased to 39 per cent in 1995 and 44 per cent by 2001.

The average Australian male is now about five kilograms heavier than he was 20 years ago, while 'Mrs Average' is tipping the scales at an extra four kilograms. The other day I read a newspaper article in which it was predicted that by 2050 every Australian will be obese.

There's a thought.

We're almost the fattest nation on earth (closing in on the United States) ... scary.

So why is it that in such an enlightened and educated age, we are becoming collectively fatter? Why do we seemingly know what to do but consistently fail to do it?

These are issues that we will explore in this book.

I hope that within these pages there will be a moment for you; a point where a light comes on and you start to find the answers that you have been searching for.

But first a warning: sometimes the answers you need to find are not the ones you want to hear or the ones you will be comfortable with.

DON'T DREAM IT, DO IT

If you have picked up this book then I am guessing that from time to time (possibly all the time) you struggle with the whole body thing (weight loss, fat loss, fitness, confidence, appearance, motivation, etc). I am also guessing that your personal struggle to create the type of body you truly desire may have been a source of frustration and, at times, significant pain and emotional distress. Join the club; it's a big one.

Since the mid-1980s I have personally completed more than 35,000 personal training sessions.

That's a lot of talking about fat bums and legs I can tell you!

My company completes about 1000 personal training sessions per week. When it comes to people trying to change their body, there is not much I haven't seen or heard.

Based on 20 years' experience of helping people get in shape, it is my firm belief that most of us can create significant change in a relatively short period of time only if we approach the process of creating that physical change with the right mindset, adequate resources and an appropriate plan.

In this book we will explore the relationship between the mind (attitude, thinking, beliefs, fears, expectations, etc) and body, and the effect that relationship has on our ability to achieve our physical goals (whether the goal is to lose weight, build muscle, run faster or make the Olympic team).

We will also analyse how the way we think and the way we see our world can help or hinder us as we strive to create our better body.

You will discover that your body has the potential to change significantly in a matter of weeks and that it is only you who can stop it from fulfilling that potential. The human body is an incredibly adaptable organism. But even though the outside is very capable of change, the inside (the psychological and the emotional) can be a little slower to catch on. That's the key; the sooner we change our attitude and our thinking, the sooner the physical transformation will begin.

CHANGE IS A MATTER OF CHOICE

One of my goals in writing this book is to help you understand the significant role that the mind plays in the process of changing your body and creating life-long physical change.

I hope that by sharing my beliefs and experiences you will come to the realisation that in the quest for the body you have always wanted, you are your greatest resource.

You are the one who chooses between the fruit or the cake, you are the one who does or doesn't get up early to exercise and you are the one who stays with the program long term or gives up two days or two weeks into the process.

This book has been written specifically for the person who has a history of *almost getting in shape*.

It is a resource for you to use in your quest to create the new you. It is full of ideas, information, thoughts, strategies, stories, motivation and inspiration. Reading it can be a life-changing experience but only if you make the necessary changes and decisions and apply the information. I suggest that as you read you use a highlighter, take notes and share what you learn with others as you go.

This way it is more likely to sink in and begin to have a life and body-changing impact. Do your best to read the book with a completely open mind and be prepared to make some tough decisions.

IT'S UP TO YOU

This book was born in part out of frustration; having been in the fitness and weight-loss business for years, I came to the point where I realised that for many people, succeeding with fitness and weight loss goals is more about attitude, clear thinking, emotions, beliefs, expectations, fears, conditioning and state of mind, than it is about dumbbells, exercise bikes and diets.

This realisation brought me to a point where I had to acknowledge that my technical and academic knowledge (about nutrition, exercise and physiology) may not necessarily help me achieve results with people. What is the point of providing somebody with the correct information and the appropriate resources to be able to create change if two weeks into the program they have thrown in the towel because it was 'too hard' or they 'got bored' or 'they couldn't see the results'?

I've learned that creating permanent change is more about psychology than physiology; developing the mind, not just the body. It struck me after a long period of observation and self-analysis that I must be doing something wrong because the people I was working with as their trainer, consistently seemed to achieve mediocre results, at best.

After a year or two it began to dawn on me that achieving outstanding results was more about empowering my clients to take complete control of their body, their habits, their behaviours, their thinking and their life, than it was about prescribing the 'right exercise program'.

Over the past 10 years I have been inspired to explore why two people given the same opportunities, the same information and the same resources will invariably achieve totally different outcomes – one succeeds, and one fails.

Let's say two people have the same ability and the same opportunity; one person will complain constantly, make excuses, be mad at the world and blame everything and everyone for their failures while the other person approaches the same challenge with a no-fuss attitude and consequently turns their life and body around in a relatively short period of time.

Every single day the first personality above makes the process of getting in shape much harder than it needs to be. The second succeeds.

So, who will change that body of yours? You will. I will help you, but it's ultimately up to you.

Trainers, doctors, psychologists and dieticians – and books like this – are resources only; helpers on the path to your goals. The sooner we stop looking for someone or something to fix us, the sooner we'll move closer towards achieving our goals and creating lasting physical change.

This book isn't going to hold your hand, confirm for you that life is not fair and it will all be okay tomorrow. This book will not reveal some previously unknown scientific fact about an exotic fat-burning herb from the Amazon, a previously unknown secret about glycemic index or give you another 'world-first' scoop on carbohydrates or protein.

It does not outline the 'seven secret steps' to physical perfection in just seven minutes a day. Not at all ... within these pages you will discover honest, insightful, relevant and practical information, based on real-life situations and real people. If used properly, it will help you create a better body. The body you want to create.

KNOW, THEN DO

For most of us, changing our bodies is not so much about a new program or new diet as it is about creating a new way of thinking and a new reality.

It is not just about knowing; it is about knowing and doing. Action and consistency are paramount. There are many ways that we can change our body and there is no single 'best' exercise program or eating philosophy, despite what many people preach.

However, certain principles work consistently and can be incorporated into virtually any program – principles and variables such as discipline, attitude, commitment, consistency, expectations, emotions, standards, motivation and beliefs will have a far greater impact on the eventual outcome; an outcome in which you not only achieve your goals and create change, but change that is forever.

A new body for life.

IN SUMMARY

- Despite all the information, education and resources, we're getting fatter as a nation.
- You've bought the book, so I know you're interested in changing your body and your habits.
- Change can happen, but you must stick to the program.
- Who chooses between the fruit and the chocolate cake? You do.
- It's not about knowing, it's about doing.
- Getting your body in shape is largely about your head!

CHAPTER 2

JUMBO

It all began for me at secondary school. I was a fat kid, who wanted to change ... and I did.

If you were a fat kid then you would be well aware of the pain that can come from being twice as big as everyone around you. Until I was about 14 years old I was an obese child. I dreaded sports days. Probably my all-time least favourite event was the infamous annual swimming carnival. Let me paint the picture.

First year of secondary school 1976 – there's a fat 13-year-old kid in the farthest corner of the change room doing his best to disrobe without actually revealing any of his ample physique.

He wears a baggy t-shirt to the pool area because he's 'sensitive to the sun'.

"Get the shirt off, Harper," the teacher says.

Begrudgingly he peels the shirt off, walks out to join his schoolmates and hugs his own waist as if that will make his rolls invisible.

Trying to find a positive, the kid rationalises that his incredibly buoyant body might help him avoid last place. It doesn't.

He flounders around the pool for 50 metres and then hoists himself out of the water well after everyone else. He then heads straight to the kiosk to console himself with a pie and a Big M (the staple diet).

Public humiliation. Exactly what us fat, insecure kids are into. Standing on the starting blocks with your stomach cascading over your bathers, knowing that you are going to come last by 10 metres doesn't really do a lot for the confidence or self-esteem. Occasionally I'd try the old 'Sir, I think I've torn my hamstring' line, only to receive the 'sure Jumbo, get on the blocks' line.

Yep, I really got pumped up for sports days.

In Grade 4, I was given the nickname of Jumbo, which stayed with me until I was into my 20s. When people address you as 'Jumbo', that label becomes your identity. You believe you are Jumbo and it is difficult to see yourself as anything else. Not only was I known as Jumbo to the kids, but also to the teachers and the parents of my friends.

When I eventually started to play football (badly), the coach and many of the players didn't even know my real name. Looking back at those years I can smile and keep it in perspective, but as a kid, learning, growing and trying to figure out how and where you fit in, a negative label can be a major emotional and developmental setback.

When you are a kid you are like a sponge. Not only are you learning in the classroom but you learn from your environment, your family and your friends. Your personality, self-esteem, confidence, beliefs, values, standards, expectations and fears are all being developed and influenced. It is little wonder that we have 40 and 50-year-olds still dragging around emotional baggage and pain from 30 years earlier.

If this is you, then there needs to be a point where you can let it go – even if it's not comfortable to do so. We all have experienced pain in the past, some more than others. While it is okay to acknowledge past pain, it isn't okay to be handicapped by it for the rest of your life. What is crucial, in terms of achieving goals and creating change, is what we do from today, not what has happened in the past. The only thing we can influence is our future and the only thing we can change about our past is the way we let it affect us now. Too many people are paralysed by their past.

Don't base your expectations and hopes for the future on what you have or haven't achieved until now. Your history is not usually a great indication of what is possible for you in the future. It's what you make of today and tomorrow that counts.

THE TURNING POINT

In secondary school I attended a private boys' college with a reasonably heavy emphasis on sport. For most of Year 7 we had compulsory weekly cross-country runs. At about 168 centimetres (5'6") and 90 kilograms (14-stone) you can imagine that I was the ultimate endurance running machine!

Consistency was my thing. Week in, week out, I would come 130th out of 130 kids. I pioneered the cross-country shuffle. It wasn't pretty but it was efficient. My format was jog 50 metres, walk 500. It worked for me.

Just before the end of Year 8 something happened. I don't exactly know why, maybe it was girls, maybe it was my desire to not come 130th any more, but I do know that I arrived at the point where I hated what I looked like with a passion and I was really, really, really ready to change.

I emphasise 'really' because since then, I've discovered many people say they want to change but they are not genuinely ready to make the sacrifices or do whatever it takes to create the change they desire. Everything has a cost and we need to decide if we are prepared to pay that price and make the necessary sacrifices. If you want a great body but you are not prepared to give up anything, get uncomfortable or make any changes, then get another goal.

One day a switch went on for me and I really, really, really did not want to be Jumbo any more. When we are genuinely ready to change we will find a way. I know I did. Sometimes it comes down to how much you want to change.

Day one of the new Craig saw me running around the soccer field across the road from my house. I ran in jeans, a blue jumper and desert boots because I didn't own a tracksuit or running shorts and I didn't know what I was doing. It wasn't pretty, but it was a start.

I think I ran about 300 metres non-stop and almost 'died'. That was my first ever 'training' experience. Little was I to know that this would be the first of thousands of workouts for me.

While I had no idea about nutrition or exercise and I was essentially making it up as I went, for the first time in my life I was absolutely passionate and driven to achieve a goal. The light was on!

Much of my early training consisted of running. The more I ran the better I felt. The better I felt, the further and faster I ran. It was an incredible experience for me to be doing something that I thought I couldn't do. Fat kids don't run, do they? My body started to change within weeks and the more it changed, the more excited I got and the easier it was for me to maintain momentum.

I didn't know anything about nutrition from a scientific perspective but even as a kid I figured out less food was better, so I essentially restricted my calories by eating less. Not rocket science, I didn't know what protein, fat and carbohydrates were or did but I inadvertently created an effective eating plan for myself and stuck to it religiously.

Despite my teenage ignorance, or because of it, over the next five months I managed to lose about 25 kilograms, dropping from 90 to 65 kilograms with virtually no help from anyone. No expensive runners, no mentor, no flash gym equipment and no whiz-bang weight-loss supplements, just youthful enthusiasm and an incredible desire to transform my body and my life.

I had made a discovery which would stay with me forever: Enthusiasm, desire and commitment are often more important than the actual program design.

While the obvious external changes were taking place, there was also a major internal metamorphosis going on. It was amazing when I started to realise that many of the things I had believed until that point in my life (about what was possible for me) didn't have to be true. They were only true if I let them be true.

I created my own reality. Maybe I could be an athlete. Maybe I could run. Maybe I could be popular. Maybe I could be attractive to someone. It might seem silly now but when you're a kid, and often as an adult, these can be major issues.

All of a sudden it dawned on me that if I was disciplined and I did certain things, I could create new habits, change my body, change my reality, change my social status (important when you're a teenager) and change my life.

Although I didn't articulate it so eloquently at 14, this was essentially what I had figured out.

ENJOY THE RESULTS

At some stage in the Year 9 sports curriculum, the infamous cross-country run made a return to the program. The second time around wasn't such a terrifying or depressing experience for me.

I can assure you that winning felt a whole lot better than finishing 130th! Every time we did a run I would either win or place in the top few, not because I was talented but because I was probably the only kid in the school who actually followed some type of structured training program.

I remember feeling things that I had never felt before. I remember people treating me differently and speaking to me differently. It was weird for me. I remember the absolute disbelief on my sports teacher's face. It was all worth it.

Just as significant as the change taking place in my body was the radical re-adjustment going on in my head. Even as a 14 year-old kid I was beginning to realise how we hide in our safe little boxes and limit ourselves.

We figure out early on, based on our life experiences, what we are and what we're not, what is possible or probable for us and what isn't.

I didn't know it, but I was learning about how we get programmed to see ourselves and our world in a certain way, how we limit our belief in ourselves, and how limiting that is for our personal growth. It's a vicious cycle.

My world and my perspective were absolutely being turned upside down. I'd busted the cycle. Once I understood that a fat kid could become an athlete I started to wonder what else was possible, and I realised that thinking and behaviour were the drivers which would make me my own worst enemy or my own best friend.

We're all the same. So many of us spend our entire lives not fulfilling our potential. We stay in the safe, comfortable boxes we have created for ourselves.

If you want to thrive and not just survive in this life, then you need to be constantly adapting and changing. We must extend ourselves and jump out of the comfort zone.

Growth usually involves a level of discomfort, so if we want to progress from where we are then occasionally we need to deal with a little pain and adversity. This doesn't mean that our life needs to be a constant battle; what it means is that in order for us to achieve what most people don't, we need to be prepared to do what most people won't – take risks (physical and emotional), make decisions, make sacrifices, be disciplined, get uncomfortable and do it consistently over time. You can relate this philosophy to almost all aspects of creating your better body.

There will be doubts, questions.

What if I fail? What if I get no support? What if I can't do it?

At times you will need to make tough decisions; 'I will exercise four days every week no matter what obstacles get in my way.'

At times there will be sacrifice; 'I will give up beer for three months ... aaah!'

There must be discipline; 'I will exercise even when I don't feel like doing it; I will make time even when it is tough to do so.'

You will need to deal with discomfort because getting uncomfortable and stretching yourself is how you cause your body to change. For most of us, merely changing our diet will cause a level of discomfort.

And, of course, we need to do these things consistently because we want to be in shape forever, not just for a few months.

I was a fat teenager.

I hated it.

I got to the point where I had to change. It wasn't a matter of 'I want to lose weight', it was 'I'm going to reinvent myself, no matter what'.

IN SUMMARY

- My story is the same story for many.
- I hated what I was and became determined to change.
- My goal was my driver, I had no real idea how to get there.
- I ran and ran, and the more I did it, the better I felt.
- I decided if I ate less, I would lose weight. I did.
- Enthusiasm will always win out. Don't let it go.
- Don't necessarily believe all the things you've been programmed to believe. Question things.
- It won't always be easy, but it'll always be worth it.
- The biggest thing that limits us, is us.

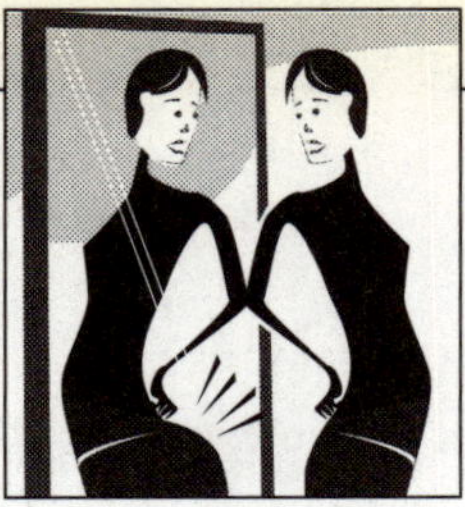

CHAPTER 3

QUESTION YOUR BELIEFS

'We don't see things as they are,

we see things as we are.'

– Anais Ninn

I often talk to people who are controlled by fear and destructive beliefs which limit their potential just like I was. 'I can't do this, I can't do that'. 'My brother's the athletic one, not me'. 'I'm fat, my dad's fat, my mum's fat, everyone in my family is fat; it's a genetic thing'.

"Hmmm," I say, "maybe your whole family eats too much!"

I have heard it all. Every day people bombard me with reasons why they can't get in shape. It always seems to be some factor beyond their control. Here's the first and last limiting factor for not achieving: if you want to find a reason why you can't or won't change, you will find one. If you really want to, you can justify anything and you can talk yourself into or out of pretty much anything.

Just because you believe something doesn't mean it is true, it just means you believe it. I am forever talking to people who believe things that are absolutely untrue because it makes them more comfortable about their situation and doing what they're doing (destructive behaviours).

If they tell me 'it's just my genetics', then they believe it, and decide it's not worth attempting change because there's obviously no hope to achieve the outcome they want.

Most of us have limiting beliefs about food, exercise, our body and what is possible for us (our potential). Just because you have never had a great body does not mean you can't have one. Just because you have never run a marathon does not mean you don't have the potential to do it one day. It just means you haven't done it ... yet.

Imagine if we only focused on what we can achieve rather than dwelling on what we can't. What would we achieve then?

I recently spoke to an overweight woman who told me that she didn't like to run or ride a bike because it made her legs bigger. The same woman also told me that she could eat as many lollies as she wanted to because they had no fat in them. Interesting beliefs.

I explained to her (patiently) why she was wrong on both counts and she told me that it was me who was wrong and that I didn't understand her body.

She didn't want to learn or to acknowledge that she might be mistaken because it would mean she would have to change. She was comfortable with her beliefs. Nobody could change them or her. The outcome: she will continue to live in a body which is less than her ideal. She will stay fat. Don't let your stubbornness, attitude or beliefs stop you from fulfilling your potential.

I regularly speak to people who have good bodies, yet they sit in my office and pour their heart out because they believe they are too fat and their body is hideous.

Where do these crazy beliefs and this type of thinking come from? How can someone who is obviously not fat, believe they are fat?

Everyone has their own reality when it comes to their body. Unfortunately, sometimes we make it harder than it needs to be. Sometimes we lose, or never had, the ability to make an objective, logical assessment about our body or our ability. Here's an example:

A few months ago, Kristin came to see me and informed me that she wanted to trim down. In her late 30s and in relatively good shape, she told me that she 'just wanted to tone up a little and lose some flab off her stomach'.

We had a chat and I explained my philosophy to her. I discovered that when she was younger she had been overweight and had always had an aversion to sport or exercise of any description.

She told me that she had never been to a gym and that it had taken her six months of driving past my business to build up the courage to walk in the door. As it turned out, there was no trainer available to take her for her first workout at her preferred time.

As I had no commitment at that time, I told her I would take her for her debut session and I would then hand her over to one of my trainers. She seemed happy with that arrangement.

We did a basic assessment, took a few measurements, set a few goals, discussed some relevant issues and headed into the gym. After a very low-key warm-up and gentle stretch, I informed Kristin that we were going to do a 200-metre slow jog (two laps of the indoor running track), have a rest and then maybe do it again. Her response was to tell me that she couldn't run.

"You told me you don't have any injuries," I said.

"I don't.

"So how come you can't run?

"I just can't.

"Everyone can run.

"Not me."

I later found out that Kristin had never been for a run, not even for a hundred metres. Ever! She told me that when she was growing up she had never played active games and could not remember running more than 50 metres. It struck me as strange that she was absolutely adamant that she couldn't run – her reality. Her limiting belief.

Not wanting to stand there and argue about it, I reached across, grabbed her hand, began to jog and started to pull her along the running track.

"What are you doing?" she asked.

"Teaching you to run," I said.

Before she realised it she had run 100 metres holding my hand (it was a bonding moment).

After the first lap I let go of her hand and told her she had one more lap to do. As we were nearing the 200-metre mark, she asked me if we could do one more lap! All of a sudden this woman who couldn't run ended up running 300 metres in one hit.

At the end of her triumphant 300-metre run I could see that something had started to happen. Kristin was ecstatic; I could see her mind racing. We had a little breather and I was about to take her to a rowing machine when she asked me if we could run some more! Realising that this was more about the psychological than the physiological, I decided to adjust the program that I had planned.

Although it was a somewhat unorthodox first session, Kristin ran 1.2 kilometres in her first-ever workout; not bad for someone who could not run. At the end of the session she was excited, visibly excited. She told me that she wished she hadn't waited so long to start exercising.

About 30 minutes after I finished with her I received a phone call from a man who introduced himself as Kristin's husband. "Did my wife really run 1.2 kilometres?" he asked me. Kristin was so excited she had rushed home to tell her husband. The change in her had begun.

So, what can we learn from stories like Kristin's?

What was the thing that changed in her from pre-workout to post-workout?

Was it her ability? No.

Was it her skill level? No.

Was it her fitness? No.

It was her belief system, her expectation, her thinking, her reality. Her understanding of herself and her potential.

It wasn't that she couldn't run. She could always run. Not necessarily far or fast, but she could run. We all do what Kristin did in different areas of our lives. Most of us base our beliefs about what is possible for us on what we have or have not achieved. Unless you are an exception, you have beliefs right now which hold you back and stop you from achieving all that you could and from fulfilling your potential. If you had no fear and no limiting beliefs, what could you achieve? You'd be amazed.

Remember: what you have achieved until now is usually no indication of what is possible for the rest of your life. It is my belief that in terms of absolute potential, most of us don't have a clue about what is really possible for us.

The biggest thing that holds us back is not ability, potential or opportunity. Most times it is fear, attitude, limiting beliefs and negative re-inforcement.

Most times it's us.

BELIEFS ... WHERE DO THEY COME FROM?

Have you ever wondered where your beliefs came from? Do you remember a point in your life where you decided that 'these are my beliefs' or did they just sort of develop independently?

The truth is that most of us rarely make conscious decisions about what we will and won't believe. Whether or not you like it or are aware of it, right now you have beliefs and thinking which may hold you back and may stop you from realising your potential.

Some people believe that they are fat and useless because that is the message their environment and their life-situation has been sending them. If you are constantly told something about yourself, pretty soon that will become your reality.

The good news is that you can change your reality. If you grew up a Catholic (like me), went to mass every week, went to Catholic schools and did the whole First Holy Communion thing, there is a fair chance by about the age of 13 or 14 you were about as Catholic as can be.

Why? Was it because you explored all the different religions, weighed it all up and based on your research and experiences made an educated and informed decision that the Catholic Church and what it represents, was for you? No, more than likely you are Catholic because your mum and dad are. Not because you ever made an independent decision.

I am not saying that we should leave our church, temple or synagogue; I am saying don't vote Liberal because your dad does. I am saying sometimes we need to stop, step back from our lives and question some of the beliefs we have had forever. Maybe our beliefs and how we see the world are part of the problem. Don't just accept other people's beliefs or values without making independent, thoughtful decisions for yourself.

If you are like most people you have firmly entrenched beliefs about yourself, your potential and your future. These may have stopped you from growing and achieving as you could and should.

Remember, the world according to us can often be a pretty distorted place and provide us with a very narrow perspective. It is difficult to expect to achieve things that you have never seen or believed possible for yourself. Just because you haven't experienced it yet doesn't mean it can't be your reality in the future.

Many Australians have eaten badly for 20 years. Just because you have always done something a certain way, don't assume it is the best way. What our parents and grandparents considered to be a 'good healthy feed' is sometimes quite the opposite.

A key to progress in this book, and for your goals to become reality is to question yourself.

Start here:

1. Where did my beliefs come from?
2. Do my beliefs enable and empower me, or do they hold me back?
3. What could I achieve if I had a more optimistic view of my potential?

IN SUMMARY

- Just because you believe something, doesn't mean it's true, it just means you believe it.
- Question your 'beliefs': there might be a better way.
- The rewards of change are far-reaching, believe it.
- Anything's possible, if you believe it's possible.
- If you expect to fail, you probably will.

CHAPTER 4

IT'S ALL ABOUT ATTITUDE

The first thing you need to change is not your diet or exercise regime; the first thing you need to change is your attitude.

For most of us, an attitude change is a pre-requisite to creating permanent physical change:

'I hate jogging, jogging's boring.' Negative.

'I don't have the time to spend stroking my ego in a gym like he does.' Negative.

'It's not fair, she eats whatever she wants and look at her body, while I eat nothing and I explode at the hips.' Negative.

'If God had wanted me to exist on rabbit food, I would have been made a rabbit.' Negative.

'As if I need to exercise … I have enough pain in my life.' Negative.

'I've tried it all, nothing works.' Negative.

As an exercise scientist, I have heard it all. Every reason in the book of negativity.

Some people who come and see me have already decided why and how they are going to fail before they have even started. It makes the inevitable less painful. They continually look for the 'easy' option hoping that someone will come along and fix their body, or conjure up the outcome they want. They tell themselves that they deserve this piece of chocolate cake (hamburger, ice-cream) and that they will start next Monday.

Of course, next Monday never comes.

Having observed people complain, whinge, make excuses, lie, procrastinate, blame others and spend years waiting for the magical right time, I can tell you with some certainty that if you really want to change your body you must also change how you look at things.

Remember, for many of us the psychological change is much more of a challenge than the physiological change.

Here's a typical experience of mine:

> A lady comes to see me because it is her daughter's wedding in six weeks. She tells me that she has six weeks to lose 15 kilograms (an unhealthy and unrealistic goal) and that she is prepared to do pretty much anything.
>
> Why, at this significant point in her life, is she prepared to do pretty much anything? Because for the next six weeks she has the necessary motivation to do what needs to be done (i.e. she doesn't want to look fat on her daughter's special day).
>
> So off she goes; six weeks of exercising, eating less, drinking water, abstaining from alcohol (and even chocolate) and seemingly doing all the right things. But, and it is a big but (excuse the pun), while the proud mother of the bride is doing all the right things for her body, guess what's happening inside her head?
>
> Is she thinking, 'Hey, this is great, once the wedding is over I'm going to maintain these new-found behaviours because I know long-term this is what is best for my body?'
>
> I don't think so. More than likely the internal dialogue is probably more like 'this is rubbish, I can't wait for this

wedding business to be over so that I can go back to being normal.' Normal, of course, means following the same unhealthy lifestyle and habits that created the very body she now desperately *needs* to change.

When I have worked with people in situations such as the wedding scenario, I find my biggest challenge is to get the person to continue these new behaviours beyond the six-week period.

This is often very difficult because while people (like our wedding lady) will change their behaviour (be positive) for a short time, for an 'event', they won't change their underlying attitude and are, therefore, subconsciously waiting for that 'event' to be over, so they can return to 'normal'.

This is the problem. We need to stop thinking short term and know that it is about the rest of our life, not about the wedding (or any similar 'event'). We need to stop getting in and out of shape. We need to commit to the big picture and understand that it won't necessarily be easy in the beginning, but it will be in the end. Getting in shape won't always be fun or entertaining – we can't be precious, we can't expect things to happen by themselves. We must make them happen, and we must believe that change is possible. If you start the process with a bad attitude, you are wasting your time.

IN SHAPE FOREVER – CREATING PERMANENT CHANGE

As a society, we are perpetually putting on and losing weight, starting and stopping programs and diets. Many of us have resigned ourselves to the fact that it is normal and acceptable to go through this cycle of increasing and decreasing our girth over the course of a year.

We even have wardrobes with 'fat' and 'skinny' sections because we know that our body size and shape will probably change significantly depending on the time of year, the upcoming social calendar and the state of mind we are in.

Unless you want to be riding the weight loss merry-go-round and alternating between the fat, skinny and medium bodies for the rest of your life, you must get to a point where you say 'enough!' Emotionally and psychologically, you need to arrive at that place where you say, 'that's it, I'm sick of wasting time and making the same mistakes'.

You need to get to that point where you say this is going to be a forever thing – this is the new me. This is not another phase I am going through. I am going to change my habits, my lifestyle, my thinking and my reality. Forever. I'm going to create new habits.

Quite often we see people who have been unable to lose weight (men and women) for much of their lives achieve the previously unachievable for that 'special day'. They seem to miraculously produce a 'never-seen-before' body and peak like an elite athlete for 'the big one' (this in itself tells us that virtually anyone can create outstanding results if there is enough reason to do so).

I worked with a lady who wanted to look fantastic on her wedding day, which is a pretty normal aspiration, and by the time the big day came around she looked great.

In the course of her three-week honeymoon she gained (are you sitting down) 10 kilograms. She went from eating five small meals per day to one large meal (for 15 hours) and from six days per week of exercise to zero days per week.

Why did she do this?

Because her 'new found' eating and exercise behaviours weren't habits, they were just things she did for a little while to look good on a certain day. When that day came and went, so did the behaviours.

Does this sound familiar?

WHEN YOU ARE REALLY READY FOR PERMANENT CHANGE, YOU WILL KNOW

The question we really need to ask ourselves is 'do I want to change my body enough?'

Or, 'do I want to change my body only if I don't need to put myself out too much?'

It is my belief that anyone can change their body significantly – and maintain it – if it is important enough to them. I have worked with people who have transformed their bodies in a matter of months – and maintained it.

These were not people who were genetically superior; they did not have some secret weapon. Rather they were people who had arrived at a point in their lives, emotionally and psychologically, where they were genuinely ready to change.

They realised that getting in shape is not always fun. Sometimes it's plain boring. They put up with a little boredom. If being a bit bored periodically meant that they might live longer or have a better body, they were prepared to put up with it and to change their attitude.

A bit of boredom or discomfort from time to time is far less painful than constantly living in a body that you hate.

Having lived in a body which was a constant source of embarrassment, I know this for a fact. When it comes to changing your body and your life you may not always enjoy the process but you will enjoy the outcome. So keep your eyes on the goal and deal with process the best you can. Be positive. You might not love the exercise, but you will love the results.

The other day I was training a guy who is trying to lose a few pounds. He has been training with me for about six weeks. At the start of the session I asked him to warm-up on one of the bikes in the gym. His opening comment for the day was, "I hate the bike. The bike is boring." I replied, "That's okay, start pedalling anyway." He looked at me with disbelief and begrudgingly started to pedal. I explained to him that if he wanted to be entertained he should see a movie or go to a concert. If he wanted to get in shape he should listen to his trainer and approach every session with a great attitude. I don't mean to sound too Sergeant-Major when I relate this story, but my point is that many of us are far too precious and if it is not going to be entertaining, easy or fun then we're not interested. Guess what? Sometimes getting in shape is not fun or entertaining but the good news is that getting in shape can be one of the most enjoyable and rewarding experiences when we approach it the right way. If you decide it will be a miserable experience, it probably will be.

IN SUMMARY

- Negativity leads to nothing doing.
- Think forever, not for now.
- When you're really ready to change, you will.
- It's not always fun doing, it's fun succeeding.
- Changing for a short time is a waste of time.
- You've proven you can change, why not make it forever.

CHAPTER 5

MOTIVATION AND INSPIRATION

We find reasons to succeed, and to fail. Success requires inspiration: failure is easy.

Motivation. I am sick of this word. It is so over-used and misunderstood; motivational speakers, motivational books, motivational tapes, motivational shops.

These days motivation is big business.

We have all these resources and yet many of us struggle to remain motivated when it comes to our exercise and our eating habits. For some people motivation can be the difference between incredible success and heart-wrenching disappointment.

So what is motivation?

For most people motivation is a feeling, an emotional state.

These two words, motivation and feeling, are often found in the same sentence. 'After I watch the Olympics I feel motivated and I go for a run.'

The problem with motivation being a feeling is that feelings can change day-to-day, or even minute-to-minute. If motivation for us is purely emotional and we rely on that emotion to reach our goals, then our day-to-day exercise and eating behaviours will be inconsistent at best.

It is crucial that we discipline ourselves to do the things we need to do on a daily basis irrespective of how we feel (how motivated we are). Within a short period of time those forced behaviours will start to become habits and the whole process will become easier and more enjoyable.

Motivation needs to be a decision and a commitment, not a feeling. 'Irrespective of how I am feeling, I will be motivated'. If you lose motivation and typically go through periods where you can't be bothered, that doesn't make you a loser, that makes you normal.

I often *feel* like staying in bed rather than going for a run, I do the run anyway.

More important than motivation is inspiration.

Inspiration is what keeps us going on the days when the 'feeling' of motivation is not there.

People who transform their bodies are usually inspired. Inspired from within. People who are inspired have a vision, a quiet determination and a focus which separates them from the majority who spend year after year getting on and off the weight loss merry-go-round and alternating from 'in the zone' to 'don't care' on a daily basis.

If you're not inspired right now, then get inspired. Here's a crazy concept: When you're not motivated to exercise, exercise anyway.

Do it because it's the right thing to do for your body and because you need to do it to achieve your goals. Sometimes we do certain things, not because it is fun or exciting, but because it is what is required to achieve our goal.

If I only exercised when I felt motivated, I would be as big as a house. There are many days when I don't feel like exercising but I do it anyway because I love what the habit of exercising has done for my body, my mind and my life.

The long-term benefits of a healthy lifestyle and a fit lean body far outweigh the short-term pleasure of a 'pig-out' and an extra 30 minutes in bed when you should be at the gym or pounding the pavement.

Unfortunately we are an instant gratification society. We want pleasure and we want it now. We want results now! Once our new lifestyle and behaviours become habits then in the long term motivation becomes less of a factor.

When it is habitual, it is something we do automatically. We don't rely on the feeling of motivation.

DO WHAT'S RIGHT FOR YOU

I have what is called an endomorphic body type; that is, I am genetically predisposed to gain bodyfat more easily than many people.

What this means in practical terms for someone like me is that I need to make sure I don't go crazy with my food intake and that I exercise regularly.

What I have discovered over the years is that running works well for me (in terms of staying lean and looking how I want to). If you ever meet me you will know I am not built like a runner. My background is bodybuilding and I am no gazelle.

Do I like running? Not a whole heap. Do I feel like running? Not often. But what I do like are the benefits I get from running. If it was simply a matter of doing what I prefer, I would stay in the gym, hang out with the lads, lift heavy things and eat two chickens for lunch.

Having tried this, I know that it's not the success formula for me to achieve the body I want. Sometimes what will be the most effective thing for our body is not going to be our preferred exercise option.

> Not too long ago I was talking to a client who trains at one of my centres. At the time she had a six-month-old baby and

was trying somewhat unsuccessfully to get back in shape. She told me that she just didn't enjoy exercise the way other people seemed to.

We were discussing the motivation thing and she asked me how I stay motivated. I told her my philosophy (she had a spare five hours) and then I asked her if she struggled to find the motivation to change those smelly nappies five times a day.

She looked at me strangely and said "I don't think about it, it's not really an issue." I asked her why it wasn't an issue and she informed me that it was just something that had to be done and that she had no choice. It took her a moment, but that light bulb came on. "I know where you're going with this," she said. "Okay I get your point."

Isn't it funny how when we have no choice, we have no motivational problems? If you make a 'you rule' that whatever standard you set yourself (exercise three times per week, for example) is not optional, you will have less motivational problems – but you need to be serious about it. Don't make wishy-washy decisions that you won't follow through on.

Create for yourself some rules that are do-able and effective.

I have a 'Craig rule' that at least six days per week I will do 30 minutes of cardiovascular exercise. It might be a run, a bike ride or a swim (I swim like a cat) but I will make sure I do something.

It is what my body needs and it keeps my mind focused – this is important also. By the way, if you are a terrible runner or swimmer I have some good news for you, the worse your technique is, the more energy you use per unit of time. So if you are not that pretty to watch in the pool, think of the calories you are burning!

When I think about inspired people, I often think of Mother Teresa. Most of what she did on a daily basis was not fun, comfortable or easy. In fact, much of what she put herself through over the years was incredibly difficult, painful, dangerous and exhausting.

Yet this tiny 'inspired' woman achieved truly incredible things in circumstances and situations that most of us cannot even begin to imagine.

She was able to achieve what many considered to be the unachievable with limited resources, limited support and very little money in one of the most trying situations imaginable because she had vision, faith, determination and inspiration.

In her mind, she had no choice (she was called by God to serve), therefore she had no motivational problems.

Occasionally when I think it is too tough for me, I think about the tiny saint who worked tirelessly on the streets of Calcutta and I realise how pathetic I am being.

EXTERNAL MOTIVATION, AND INSPIRATION

Sometimes inspiration is imposed on us for reasons outside our control. Here's an example:

> About 12 years ago I was sharing a house with a guy named Dave. At the time I was in one of my 'how massive can I get for no sensible reason' bodybuilding phases.
>
> Dave and I got on great but had slightly different approaches when it came to eating and exercise. His philosophy was eat whatever, whenever and avoid exercise at all costs unless it involved women.
>
> On a daily basis I would try to entice him to come to the gym but my efforts were usually in vain. Every night I would try to tempt him with a home made chicken stir-fry instead of the fine cuisine from the local fish and chip establishment around the corner.
>
> He would regularly tell me that he wished he could have the discipline and the motivation that I had. In six months

of living together he came to the gym with me about two or three times and told me it was all too hard.

I remember one day I was talking to Dave and he told me that he had been getting some pain in one of his legs for a while. He described it to me and it didn't seem to me like it was a muscular type of pain.

He went to see a doctor who also didn't really know what the problem was but decided to send him for some tests. Within a few weeks Dave had been told he had bone cancer.

In my lifetime, I have never seen such an instant turnaround in a person's behaviour , attitude and lifestyle as I did with Dave.

In the space of one day, my friend went from being a party boy with no willpower, who would eat and drink anything, to the healthiest person I knew. Within weeks he was trying to convert me to organic foods and purified water. Steady on, cowboy.

What amazed me watching him go through this process was how this guy who apparently didn't have any motivation, instantly had more motivation, discipline and self-control than I had ever had.

The good news is that Dave survived cancer, is still alive and well today and has not been to the fish and chip shop since his diagnosis.

If we really need to, we can all produce the motivation and the discipline to achieve pretty much anything. Sometimes it is not that we can't. It is that we won't, or that we haven't yet?

LEARN FROM DAVE

So, as Dave learned well, the time to make life-changing decisions is not when you are backed into a corner. Do it before you get into that corner. This might sound somewhat melodramatic, but for some of you reading this book (or someone close to you), making a significant decision today might be the difference between life and death. So don't wait for the right time to make a decision about your greatest resource.

By not making a decision, you are making a decision. You don't accidentally end up where you are. You arrive there via the decisions you do and don't make.

The time to take the first step is not next week or next month. The time to decide to do something about your body is not when you are scared or sick. The time to take action is now, before you get to that desperation point.

If I had $10 for every person who has told me that when their kids are all at school, or when it is not so cold in the morning, or when they have paid off the house, or the car, or the dog, that they will begin an exercise program and change their lifestyle, I would be a wealthy man.

For many people it will never be the right time because they don't make it the right time. We all have busy lives. We all have reasons why it is too hard to start right now.

Unlike our health, most things in life are replaceable, so why take a chance with your body? We invest so much time, energy and effort into things which, in the big picture, are really insignificant, when compared with our health and our life.

Many times I have had discussions with businessmen who put their lives in jeopardy on a daily basis because they are not ready to change. They are 'too busy'.

If only they took 10 per cent of the time and energy they use on their career and invested that in their bodies they would live longer, enjoy life more and probably achieve more at work, with less time and energy.

When we are fitter and healthier we deal with physical, mental and emotional stress more effectively, we experience less fatigue and tiredness, we are less susceptible to depression and mood swings, we experience greater levels of motivation and confidence and we are nicer people to be around!

So what are you waiting for?

IN SUMMARY

- Be disciplined: do what needs to be done.
- When you don't feel like exercising, exercise anyway.
- Stick with the program to achieve your goal.
- By not making a decision, you are making a decision.
- Don't rely on motivation, rely on positive habits.
- For many people, the right time never comes - don't be one of them.

SECTION TWO

LET'S GET STARTED

Now that you've worked out where you want to be and what you want to achieve, this section will help you on the road to change. It's all about doing, so let's get started.

Chapter 6 **A business plan – for your body** 52
A plan ... for you

Chapter 7 **The preliminaries** 56
How to set appropriate goals

Chapter 8 **Action starts here** 65
Putting ideas into action

Chapter 9 **How to eat well** 74
Some ideas on healthy eating

Chapter 10 **How to excercise well** 99
Some exercise guidelines

CHAPTER 6

A BUSINESS PLAN – FOR YOUR BODY

You're not going to 'accidentally' achieve your goals. We need to plan for success.

Being a young instructor working in a fitness club it was my job to talk to new members and perform fitness evaluations. Based on the collected information, I would design a training program to suit the client's needs, body type, goals and time availability.

As a 19-year-old I would pride myself on the quality of the programs I would write and the effort I would make to ensure that I provided every member with the program best for them.

While some instructors would churn out essentially the same program for everyone, I would do my best to design a program which was specific to the needs of each individual. I would endeavour to provide every member with the best opportunity of achieving his or her goals.

It took me about six months to realise that, as a general rule, the quality of my programs often had very little to do with the type of results (if any) achieved by each member.

Writing a program specific to an individual's needs is one thing; getting them to follow that program for more than two weeks is another! The best plan in the world is useless if it is not followed. Gyms have filing cabinets full of exercise programs which are never even taken out of the drawer.

It took me awhile to realise that some people would continually ask me for advice that they would never act upon. I couldn't understand why people would ask a question, I would give them the answer and then they would go away and ignore my advice.

Maybe I didn't give them the answers they wanted to hear. That's why I wrote this book. It's a collection of two things – all the reasons people succeed. All the reasons they fail.

Having resources and information is good. Using those resources and that information is even better.

If you decide to join a gym or buy a piece of exercise equipment, make sure you follow through with your intentions. Joining a gym isn't what gets results. Going to the gym consistently and diligently for the entire length of your membership is what counts. Buying an exercise bike is easy. Using it consistently over time (even when you can't be bothered) is not so easy.

I am sure people join fitness centres just so they can say they have a gym membership. Sometimes we don't really want to make an effort; we just want to look like we are making an effort. It's a good way to get people off our back.

If you've made it this far, I know you want to succeed. In the following pages (before you get to all the reasons people give up), you'll find a business plan for change. I say business plan because changing your body and your life is just as involving and prone to variations as any business plan. I've made this easy. Please give it a go.

EXAMPLE BUSINESS PLAN

STEP 1

Identify what your key issues are right now

- Weight
- High body-fat level
- Bad posture
- High blood pressure
- Inconsistency
- Motivation
- Attitude
- Poor diet
- Unhealthy lifestyle
- Stress
- Lack of muscle/strength
- Lack of flexibility
- Energy levels

Hopefully they're not all issues!

STEP 2

In terms of health, fitness and appearance, where do you want to be in 3, 6, 12 months from now?

Make sure your objectives are clearly defined and specific. The clearer they are in your mind, the more focused you will be, the more momentum you will create and the more likely you will be to achieve your goals.

STEP 3

What's your formula – how will you get there? Having a destination is important but having a map which will take you there is crucial.

Will you use a gym?
Will you train with a friend/partner?
Will you keep a food and exercise diary?
Will you make some 'you rules'? (Every day I will ... Every week I will ...)
How will you eat?
How will you exercise?

STEP 4

What changes do you need to make to ensure you succeed?

If we always do what we've always done, we'll always achieve what we have in the past. Sometimes we need to make some significant changes if want to create 'forever' results.

STEP 5

What help do you need to get where you're going?

We all need help, encouragement, support, guidance and education at different stages of our journey. This may come in the form of a friend or partner or it may come from a professional such as a doctor, a dietician or a personal trainer.

IN SUMMARY

- It's not the program, it's what you do with it.
- Don't take out a gym membership, if you won't use it.
- Set some clearly defined goals.
- Be honest with yourself: imagine you're always on display.
- Assess what you need to do/change to achieve your goals.

CHAPTER 7

THE PRELIMINARIES

Now you're clear on your destination, turn the key and get those wheels turning.

Only you can determine where you (personally) need to start because we all have our own specific issues which are going to be 'make or break' for us. With me, for example, getting in shape and staying that way has always been largely about being in control of my eating. I personally find the exercise component relatively easy but have always found the food side much more of a challenge.

So maybe it is more of a food thing than an exercise thing for you, or maybe it is more about you managing your time better, re-assessing your priorities or changing your lifestyle.

Maybe it is about the whole lot!

Rather than telling you specifically where you should start, I have decided to provide you with a suggestion list. Some of these will be must-do items and others may not be so relevant right now. Remember there is no 'one-approach-fits-all' solution. Take what you need and use it.

A key to succeeding is for you to become more educated, more aware, more consistent, more pro-active and more personally empowered to create the type of physical changes you've desired for so long.

Don't rely (totally) on anyone else; rely on you. When clients rely totally on me, they are empowering me not them. This is going backwards not forwards.

Right now you have everything that you need to create the type of results of which you have always dreamt. It is not about any particular eating philosophy or training regime; it's about you. How you exercise and eat is an issue but it is not *the* issue. You are.

Whether or not you create the type of genuine life-long physical changes I have been describing will not have much to do with which gym you join this week or whether or not you have carbohydrates after lunch today. It will have a lot to do with the decisions you make and the things you do over the next 10 weeks, 10 months and 10 years.

Remember it is not for a few weeks; it is for a lifetime. To achieve the success you want requires an ordered process.

Being an effective decision-maker and goal-setter is extremely important if you are to successfully create the type of forever changes that I have been talking about.

Through my seminars I have discovered that while most people have at least a basic understanding of what goal setting is and why we should do it, most of us either don't set goals effectively or don't set goals at all.

In this chapter I am going to provide you with an effective goal-setting formula and some guidelines that I know can make the difference between success and failure in the pursuit of your best body. Effective goal-setting requires discipline, consistency, vision and courage.

It is not a hit or miss process.

Goals are not vague dreams and aspirations trapped somewhere deep in our subconscious. They are a clearly defined picture of what we want our future to be – a picture that creates momentum and causes us to be proactive. The following are some guidelines to help you get started:

1. Identify what has held you back in the past.

If we don't identify and deal with the things which have stopped us from succeeding and achieving in the past, we will always fall into the same trap and will never get where we want to go.

For example, if you have a history of being inconsistent, then you need to address that inconsistency before you will become an effective goal-setter and achieve the success you desire.

For many people procrastination is a major issue. If you are someone who has a history of almost doing things, then STOP STUFFING AROUND!

Fear, laziness, inconsistency, ignorance, indifference and mental and emotional weakness typically hold us back. Find out what is your stumbling block and address that first. The sooner we address the things which have held us back, the sooner we will create the results we have only ever dreamed of.

For example, there is no use spending $1000 on a gym membership if you have a trail of unused gym memberships behind you.

Create a list of what's caused you to fail. I've made a box which might help you. These are some of the reasons I've heard and seen in my 20 years in the business.

EXAMPLES OF WHY PEOPLE DON'T ACHIEVE

- Following the wrong program – (based on our age, needs, goals, fitness/strength level).
- Training too hard (over-training).
- Not training hard enough (going through the motions).
- Crappy attitude – whinge, sook, grizzle, complain, make excuses, procrastinate.
- Short-term bursts – unfortunately we need to do something for longer than two weeks if our goal is permanent change.
- We wait for the magical right time to get in shape – it never arrives.
- We only make significant health/fitness decisions when we are scared or backed into a corner.
- We get one thing right (we exercise well) and another thing drastically wrong (we eat enough for 16 people). *"I've been working out, I deserve this".*

2. Make some life-changing decisions.

Find a quiet place, take some time out and really spend time focusing on what and how you need to change over the next (fill in the number) months or years.

Resolve that another month will not pass without you creating real change (not short-term change) and making significant progress with your weight-loss/fitness goals.

Step back from your situation and identify what you don't like and what you are going to do about those issues or situations.

Make decisions that you know you should have already made but have been putting off forever, even if those decisions make you uncomfortable. Remember that for many people, the right time never comes.

If you struggle to gain clarity in the decision-making process, consider involving someone that you absolutely trust and respect to give you honest, objective and un-emotional guidance and feedback but don't let them tell you what you should be doing and don't let them make the decisions for you.

Only you should make decisions for your life. Friends should be nothing more than a sounding board to provide objective, intelligent feedback and opinion.

EXAMPLES OF LIFE CHANGING DECISIONS

- I'm going to stop smoking over the next six weeks.
- I'm only going to drink alcohol two days (not seven) per week.
- I'm going to join a gym.
- I'm going to see a professional about my eating disorder.
- I'm going to be honest about what I put in my mouth – I won't lie to others or to myself.
- I'm going to stop procrastinating and making excuses
- I'm going to do what's necessary even if it's not comfortable, even if it's not fun.
- I'm going to have a positive attitude (it's a decision we make).
- I'm going to the doctor for a full health screen (roll over knees to chest Mr Harper).
- I'm actually going to use the information in this book!

3. Make the goal-setting process a methodical one.
Set specific goals and objectives. These might be behavioural goals like eating five small healthy meals every day, or to stop smoking, or they also might be more task-oriented like aiming to complete a marathon, a five-kilometre run or a one-kilometre swim.

Set yourself a time frame so that you are under some

pressure to stay on track. If there is no time factor we tend to lose momentum.

Deadlines and checkpoints along the way can be valuable in that they help you work to a schedule and stay focused. Anything that helps you maintain momentum it is a good thing – consistency is one of the keys.

Make sure your goals are achievable but also ambitious and don't be scared to stretch yourself. If possible, make your goals measurable so that you can gauge your progress.

If it is your goal to lose weight and bodyfat then it is fundamental to have your measurements taken on the first day so that you can objectively evaluate your progress as you go.

Don't rely on your own personal judgement as the only means to assess your progress. When you look at yourself 10 times a day in the mirror it is very hard to objectively gauge genuine progress.

If you really want to get serious and have a big reality check, get in your undies and get someone to take some 'before' photos (front, side and back – yes, back!).

This isn't necessarily what we want to do but it gives you an accurate picture of what your body really looks like.

Set short, medium and long-term goals and make sure they are written down.

A GOAL SETTING PROCESS

When setting goals sometimes using the S.M.A.R.T. model is helpful

S – **Specific**
M – **Measurable**
A – **Achievable (and ambitious)**
R – **Realistic**
T – **Time based**

Instead of having a vague goal like 'I want to get in shape', we can be a lot more specific, for example:

S – SPECIFIC – I want to decrease my bodyfat levels and my bodyweight.

M – MEASURABLE – My bodyfat level is currently 35 per cent and I would like to reduce it to 25 per cent. I currently weigh 72 kilos and I would like to weigh 58 kilos.

A – ACHIEVABLE – Is it achievable for me to reach those targets? Yes because I've been there before and I know I was fit and healthy then. Is it ambitious? Yes because I know it's going to be tough at times.

R – REALISTIC – Is it realistic for me (based on my age, genetics, time frame)? Yes because I've spoken to a professional and I was advised that my goals are realistic for someone of my age and body type.

T – TIME BASED – Considering a healthy rate to lose weight is about 0.5 to 1 kilo per week, I am giving myself a time frame of 20 weeks to lose the weight and bodyfat. So that means on the 5th of July (for example) I will be at my target weight and bodyfat level.

When we start to set goals methodically and create timelines to work towards, we drastically increase our chances of creating the outcomes we desire. So ... get to it!

4. Take action, be proactive.

As soon as you have made your life- (or body-) changing decisions and have set your goals, do something straight away to bring about the realisation of those goals – now, not next week.

It may be something small like making a phone call, going for a walk, buying some low-fat milk or joining a gym, but do something today!

Make sure that you do something every day to bring you closer to where you want to be. It is not what you know; it is what you do with what you know.

EXAMPLE 'TO DO' LIST

- Throw out all of the rubbish in your pantry.
- Go shopping for some healthy replacements.
- Start to read nutritional labels – not so you become obsessed but so that you educate yourself about what you put in your mouth.
- Buy some new runners.
- Draw up a weekly schedule for your exercise plan. 'Monday I will ... Tuesday I will ...'
- Tell someone that you trust what you're up to – public commitment is good sometimes and perhaps they will keep you accountable.
- Start a food and exercise diary.

Now, sit down and design your own list.

5. Persevere – finish what you start.

The number one reason we don't achieve our better body is that many of us don't finish what we start. The best program in the world is worthless if we don't consistently follow it.

The best intentions amount to nothing and all the goals and promises about how we are going to change are ultimately just a bunch of hot air, unless we are prepared to tough it out when the novelty and the initial burst of enthusiasm wears off.

I talk to people every day who have never achieved their

goals for no reason other than they never really follow through long term with decisions that they make about their body, their exercise, their food and their lifestyle.

They perpetually start all types of programs and perpetually stop those programs for all sorts of (claimed) reasons. The real reason usually has something to do with the fact that 'it's not happening fast enough' or 'it's uncomfortable' or 'it's not fun.'

If it was easy to have a great body we would all have one. It isn't and we don't. Sometimes creating our best body and having fun are not synonomous. You will have fun once you start to enjoy the results.

IMPROVISE AND ADAPT

Invariably things will not work out exactly as we plan them. Life usually provides us with plenty of opportunities to learn.

When you encounter obstacles along the way (and you will at some stage), the important thing is how you cope with those challenges.

Don't throw in the towel. Don't use the first hurdle as an opportunity to give up. Use it as an opportunity to learn, grow and develop character. It is not what happens that matters. It is how you react to what happens that matters.

IN SUMMARY

- Identify your faults and past failures.
- Decide to change and then do it.
- Measure your progress.
- Plan wisely, and seek advice if necessary.
- Act every day.
- Adapt: things don't always go as planned.
- Stick with it.

CHAPTER 8

ACTION STARTS HERE

Knowing what to do won't create results, but doing what we know will.

Don't wait for the motivation to kick in. When you lack motivation (and you will because you are human), do it anyway. If you have read this far, you are going great. I am guessing that by about now your level of motivation is higher than it was when you started reading; unfortunately it won't be forever – that's just what happens.

Bottle the way you feel now and get moving.

On the following pages, I have listed some suggestions that might be valuable as you begin the 'action' phase of the process.

Remember, motivation can be a decision, not just a feeling.

SUGGESTION 1:

Consider getting a personal trainer or fitness coach.

This suggestion is completely optional but for some people a trainer or fitness coach can be a valuable addition to the body-changing process (at least in the early stages). A trainer can provide education, motivation, structure and accountability – for some people, a quality trainer will be a valuable asset.

While you don't want to completely rely on a trainer, they can be a valuable resource. Many people don't need one, some do.

If you are looking for someone, make sure they are appropriately qualified, experienced, insured, competent, professional and that they have good teaching and communication skills (don't demand much, do I?).

The best way to find a quality trainer is by referral, so if you have a friend who is getting great results with their trainer then that might be a good place to start.

SUGGESTION 2:
Talk to a professional.

Sometimes it is worthwhile to talk to relevant health professionals before you get under way as they may provide you with valuable information and direction specific to your body and your needs.

They may also save you from wasting precious time and prevent unnecessary frustration. Dieticians, doctors, physiotherapists, podiatrists, exercise scientists and psychologists are some of the experts who may be valuable for you to consult with from time to time. Talking to a professional may also alleviate unnecessary time-wasting and frustration.

SUGGESTION 3:
Create a realistic plan.

Goal-setting is somewhat pointless if we don't have a map to get us to where we want to go – to turn those goals into reality.

Imagine if you were going to see a long lost cousin and you had to drive to a place that you had never been to before. Let's say it is a two-hour drive and you get up early.

You are motivated, you are focused, you have a good attitude and you even have a destination (that is, you know the name of the place you are going to). The only thing you don't have is a map of how to get there.

You figure you don't need the map because you have the motivation and determination to get you there. Two weeks later you are still driving, you still don't have a map and you are actually now four days from your destination because you have been driving in the wrong direction. Seems silly, doesn't it?

As if any of us would do this. The truth is many of us do this with our bodies on a continual basis; we try to achieve that elusive best body yet we don't have a map, or if we do, we don't follow it.

Motivation and determination are important but trying to reach a destination without a map is a recipe for disappointment. The random nutritional and exercise approach does not work.

The following plan is an example only of how a person may typically approach the getting in shape process.

EXAMPLE OF A PLAN

- I will undergo a health/fitness assessment so that I have documented my starting point (this is called baseline data).
- I will eat five small healthy meals per day.
- I will eat breakfast every day.
- I will walk to work every day instead of driving (2 kms morning and night).
- I will lift weights twice a week for 45 minutes.
- I will stretch every second day for 15 minutes.
- I will play tennis twice a week.
- I will 'weigh in' once a fortnight with Sally the trainer.
- At the six-week mark I will assess my progress and adjust my program accordingly.

Remember, different things work for different people and there is no 'single best' approach or plan which will be universally appropriate for everyone. Only you really know you. So design your plan with your specific strengths, weaknesses and needs in mind. If you need help in the planning phase, enlist the help of someone suitably qualified and they may provide you with some quality direction and objectivity.

SUGGESTION 4:

Take some 'before' measurements and photos.

Ask someone to take your measurements using a tape measure (and fat callipers if you have access to them). Even though it is probably not something that you will be overly excited about, I strongly suggest that you take some 'before' photos from the front, side and back. Photos and measurements help us bring some logic and objectivity into what can sometimes be an emotional process.

While it may not be high on your 'fun things to do' list, it will provide you with an accurate picture of your body and whether or not you are progressing – the picture doesn't lie!

When you weigh yourself do it in minimal clothing (preferably not in a public place!), first thing in the morning with an empty stomach on the same scales every time so you can get an accurate indication of how you are progressing.

Weighing yourself in different clothes, on different scales at different times of the day will not provide you with an accurate indication of your progress.

When I weigh myself in the morning I weigh between 80 and 81 kilograms but when I weigh myself at night I usually weigh around the 83-kilogram mark.

Don't confuse fat with weight. A change in weight does not necessarily mean a change in body composition (how much fat and muscle we have), which is what we are really interested in.

SUGGESTION 5:
Do some shopping.

Organisation is one of the keys to a successful outcome, so get organised with your food. Throw out the junk in your pantry and your fridge and spend some quality time shopping for your new body.

Make sure you read and understand the nutritional labels and don't assume that the packaging of the product will not be misleading (e.g. *ONLY 3% FAT* ... but 45% sugar!).

SUGGESTION 6:
Work in four-week blocks.

Ease into it! Don't start something that you won't finish. With both your food and your exercise program, ease into it over the first few weeks and months. The more extreme the approach (especially in the beginning) the less likely you are to stay with it or create long-term change (your best body forever). Easy does it.

Many of the popular diets currently doing the rounds will do you more harm than good, long term, because they are not maintainable and they are unrealistic for the average person (you and I).

Many of them are based on very questionable science and work on rapid weight loss (which is usually followed by rapid weight gain).

Many people find that breaking the whole process down into four-week blocks makes it a lot easier to get their head around – remember, it is largely about your head.

While we obviously have long-term objectives, it is often much easier to work around four-week goals as we tend to stay more motivated week to week.

It is hard to stay pumped from 'day one' when we are talking about a two-year process with no objectives sighted – and achieved – along the way.

CHANGE METHODICALLY AND SENSIBLY; DON'T BE EXTREME

Anything which is extreme is more than likely not maintainable. Don't start something you know you will not maintain long term.

Make sensible, realistic, progressive changes over time. What often works best is to initially identify two or three things about your eating habits which need to be changed and over the weeks as your motivation and discipline kick in, make more changes.

Change your eating habits progressively over time and you are much more likely to maintain those changes and create results which last – that is what we are interested in. Diets don't generally work because they are extreme.

Your changes in the first few weeks might look like this:

DIET	EXERCISE
WEEK 1	
• Drink two litres of water per day • Eat breakfast every day • Change from full-cream to skim milk • Eliminate chocolate	• Walk 20 minutes per day
WEEK 2	
• Eat dinner every night before 7.30pm • Decrease the size of meals by 20 per cent • Introduce four alcohol-free days per week • Change from regular to low-fat cheese	• Add 3x10 sit-ups per day
WEEK 3	
• Remove butter, and oil from your diet • Decrease coffee from eight cups to three • Introduce two pieces of fruit per day into your diet • Reduce the sugar in your coffee from two teaspoons to one	• Increase walking to 30 minutes per day • Include push-ups (3x10)

DIET	EXERCISE
WEEK 4	
• Switch from white bread to rye bread • Switch from high sugar to low sugar cereal • Start making lunch every day rather than buying it • Increase fruit intake to three pieces per day	• Add one 30-minute bike ride per week

This four-week progression is an example of how I might progress one of my clients over the initial month. How someone should progress over the first four weeks will depend on their starting point, current habits, attitude and level of motivation.

Even if someone is very motivated it is still wise to make changes progressively, as wholesale changes made in the first month are rarely maintained.

Often when people's motivation drops off, so do the new behaviours. The four-week progression outlined above is an effective way to allow people to get their head around the process. A start. Where it ends depends on you.

SUGGESTION 7:

Keep a food and exercise diary (see Appendix).

Diarise your endeavour (at least until it becomes positive habit).

Diarise exercise, food, sleep, supplements, moods, water consumption, alcohol intake, energy levels and anything that will have a bearing on the outcome (how you look, feel and function).

For many people a diary helps keep them organised, structured, accountable and in the zone. I know it may seem somewhat obsessive to diarise everything, but just commit to do it for a month at least and you will begin to see the benefits.

SUGGESTION 8:
Train with a buddy.

Many people find exercising with a partner more motivating, stimulating and enjoyable. Most of us find that if we have a commitment to a friend (as well as to ourselves) we are more likely to stay with the program. Whatever keeps us doing what we need to do is good.

SUGGESTION 9:
Listen to your body. Watch your body.

If you learn to listen to your body (really listen), it will tell you what it needs. How many times have you said to yourself 'I'm so full' and kept on eating?

I have several friends who get drunk on a regular basis, wake up with a terrible hangover, swear they will never do that to their bodies again and then do the very same thing the following week.

Our bodies are constantly talking to us and telling us what they do and don't need. Unfortunately these are messages that we often choose to ignore.

When you struggle to walk up a flight of stairs or you are exhausted at the end of every day, your body is telling you something. Maybe it is telling you that you need more sleep or that you need to eat better and lose a few kilograms.

Maybe it is telling you that you need to do some exercise or that you are perpetually dehydrated (about half the population is regularly dehydrated). Whatever the case, your body is talking to you and I strongly suggest that you do your best to listen.

A few years ago my body began to tell me not to drink coffee any more. It did this by providing me with increasingly frequent episodes of irregular and racing heart beats.

Deep down I knew it was the coffee because an 'event' always followed a cuppa. Rationalising that it 'couldn't be the coffee' because I had been drinking coffee with no problems for 20 years, I decided to ignore my body – for a while.

When I ended up in hospital on a Saturday night with a 'resting' heart rate of 180 (about three times normal) I decided not to ignore my body any more. In five years without coffee I have had no more episodes.

Remember: your body knows, even if you don't.

SUGGESTION 10:

You might struggle, but keep going anyway.

When most people lose a little motivation they throw in the towel. If you only exercise and eat well when you feel like it, you will never get in shape because you are not going to always feel like it. So, on the days when you can't be bothered, do it anyway. It's about commitment, not motivation.

IN SUMMARY

- Good intentions won't do it, action will.
- Plan to succeed.
- Take some before and after photos.
- Occasionally it's a good idea to talk to a professional.
- Shop for success.
- Consider working in four-week blocks.
- Work out with a buddy.
- Learn to listen to your body (it knows).
- Keep a diary.
- When it's tough keep going.

CHAPTER 9

HOW TO EAT WELL

Eating well is not that difficult ... it's just that we choose not to.

While there are many excellent books on diet available, I believe there are way too many 'breakthrough' books making amazing claims that their method or philosophy is superior and 'the only way'.

I am not a dietician although I have studied nutrition extensively and talk to people on a daily basis about their diet. I have no intention of adding to the confusion that surrounds the food issue or entering into a debate over the merit of any particular 'nutritional school of thought'.

Instead, I am going to keep things simple and address the typical, everyday issues and challenges that we all face in our quest to create a leaner and more desirable body.

First, see if you can get your head around this concept:

For most people getting in shape is much more about diet than it is about exercise.

This statement is based on two decades of watching people struggle to get their eating under control. The reality is that the majority of us find it more difficult to gain complete control of our eating habits than we do to get involved in regular exercise or activity. Aussies love food; our lives revolve around it.

I have worked with many people who exercise consistently, sometimes for years on end, yet constantly struggle to gain control when it comes to their food. Even though they exercise consistently, they are invariably overweight.

I know many people who have a high bodyfat percentage, are very fit and are very consistent with their exercise habits, yet are very erratic when it comes to how and when they eat.

They train all the time, yet their eating habits vary from perfect to out-of-control in a matter of days or sometimes hours.

If you are in control of your food and your food is not in control of you then you are on your way to creating your perfect body.

NUTRITIONAL GUIDELINES AND RECOMMENDATIONS

Nutritional needs vary greatly depending on age, gender, body type, exercise habits and general activity level (this includes incidental and occupational activity). For me to write a specific eating strategy for someone that I have never spoken to (perhaps you) would be risky and irresponsible.

If you are genuinely confused about your nutritional needs or you feel that you need something written on a piece of paper 'specifically for you', then I suggest that a trip to a recommended dietician would be a worthwhile investment.

However, I also strongly suggest that you do learn to listen to your body as it knows what you need, and learn over time what works best for you.

At the risk of sounding repetitive, I cannot stress enough how important it is for you to diarise your food intake, especially if your goal is to lose weight and bodyfat.

When you diarise everything (and I mean everything) it

becomes much easier to establish what the most effective nutritional approach is for you, where you are going wrong (or right) and what changes you need to make.

These guidelines (as with any guidelines) will not be universally endorsed or embraced by every nutritional guru.

They are my recommendations and suggestions only, and are based on what I have found to be realistic, maintainable and effective for the average person trying to create their perfect body. They are based on 20 years of watching thousands of very different people trying to achieve essentially the same thing; a leaner, lighter, more functional body. Here they are:

EAT FIVE OR SIX SMALL(ISH) MEALS PER DAY

These meals should all be roughly the same size. This means that your dinner and your mid-morning meal will be about the same size. Obviously the specific size of the meals required can vary greatly from person to person. A 105-kilogram bricklayer with a fast metabolism won't have the same nutritional requirements as a 75-kilogram accountant with a slow metabolism.

So you can get your head around what I'm talking about, I thought I'd provide you with a sample of what I might typically throw down on a given day. This is not a suggested eating plan for you, it is an example only of the types of foods I consume and how I structure my eating through the day.

FIVE MEALS A DAY – AN EXAMPLE

7.00am Breakfast

20 grams of unprocessed bran, 80 grams of quick-cook oats, skim milk

One banana (the greener ones have a lower Glycemic Index)

One tea

10.00am Mid-morning
One low-fat yoghurt
One apple

1.00pm Lunch
One chicken breast and salad rye bread sandwich (no butter, marg, mayo or cheese)

4.00pm Mid-afternoon
One Protein Drink (low fat, low sugar)

7.00 – 8.00pm Dinner
Protein source (chicken, beef, turkey, fish, eggs) and vegetables

Emergency Snacks
Low-fat hot chocolate drink
Fruit
Low-fat yoghurt
Protein bar

While it doesn't always work out exactly as I intend, I do my best to stay with a structure as close to the above example as possible. Keeping in mind that we are all busy people, planning, preparation and organisation are key elements when it comes to consistently eating five to six small healthy meals per day. Every night before I go to bed I plan my menu for the following day. This might mean putting my cereal in a container to take to work, cutting up some fruit or cooking some chicken and rice. Don't be obsessed but be organised. There's nothing worse than getting to a point in your day where you are starving and you don't have access to quality food. That's the time when we begin to rationalise that a hamburger is a pretty healthy choice because it contains lettuce and the dim sim is almost vegetarian so it must be good.

EAT 40-50 GRAMS OF FIBRE PER DAY

Good in theory, but what exactly constitutes 40 grams of fibre? In order to obtain 40 grams of dietary fibre (from a single product) you would need to consume one of the following:

- 5 large mangoes
- 2 cups of kidney beans
- 80 chocolate eclairs (don't try it!)
- ½ kilo of fresh coconut
- 100 grams of unprocessed bran
- 25 cups of cooked white rice
- 5 cups of mixed dried fruit
- 80 cups of Special K (35g cups)
- 53 slices of white bread
- 12 slices of dark rye bread
- 3.5 cups of baked beans
- 12 large bananas
- 5 cups of Sultana Bran
- 20 potatoes
- 10 oranges
- 10 cups of Nutri-Grain
- 40 Mars bars

* Reference: *Fat and Fibre Counter*, Rosemary Stanton

Obviously we don't want to get our daily fibre requirements from one source nor do we want to consume all of our fibre in one hit. Do your best to consume your fibre over the course of the day. 40–50 grams of fibre in one hit will play havoc with your digestive system and probably won't do a lot for your social life!

Because the typical Australian diet is high in fat and low in fibre many people are continually plagued with digestive problems and are frequently constipated — increasing your intake of fibre will certainly help. It will also decrease your risk of bowel cancer, breast cancer, diabetes and gall stones ... so what are you waiting for? Get out there and buy some high fibre products or at the very least, some unprocessed bran. I add unprocessed bran to my cereal every morning because it's an easy way to add some quality fibre to my diet.

NO ADDED SALT ON ANYTHING

There is more than enough salt on nearly everything we buy. Less than 2000 milligrams of sodium per day is what I suggest. Just to give you an idea of how much sodium some foods contain, here's a quick snapshot for you (exact amounts will vary from brand to brand):

• 100 grams of cheese	– 600 milligrams
• 3 teaspoons of soy sauce	– 1000 milligrams
• 1 teaspoon of butter	– 25 milligrams
• 10 ml of BBQ sauce	– 75 milligrams
• 1 wholemeal pita bread (100 grams)	– 200 milligrams
• 6 Vita Wheat crispbreads (small size)	– 158 milligrams
• 100 grams of Pringles chips (sour cream and onion)	– 700 milligrams
• 2 slices of white bread	– 300 milligrams
• 100 grams of baked beans (in ham sauce)	– 380 milligrams

As you can see we certainly don't need to add any salt to our diet, so next time you feel compelled to give the salt shaker a run at the dinner table, do your best to refrain. It may take you a few weeks to really get your head and body around the decrease in salt but your taste buds will adjust (takes about a week or two) and your arteries will be applauding. I can hear them beginning to clap now.

EAT APPROXIMATELY ONE GRAM OF PROTEIN PER KILOGRAM OF BODYWEIGHT, PER DAY

So if you weigh 60 kilograms eat somewhere in the vicinity of 60 grams of protein per day.

If you are very active this can increase by as much as 100 per cent. Vary your protein sources; chicken, fish, beef, turkey, eggs, soy and dairy are all good options.

If you struggle to meet your daily protein needs you may want to use a high quality protein supplement (you can find these at any health shop or most gyms).

The following will give you an idea of how much protein some of the better sources contain. Remember, spread your protein intake over the entire day; don't eat a small farm animal at a single sitting.

• 100 grams of tuna	22 grams
• 100 grams of chicken	24 grams
• 100 grams of topside beef	32 grams
• 100 grams of tasty cheese	27 grams
• 100 millilitres of skim milk	3.5 grams
• 100 grams of baked beans	5.5 grams
• An egg	5–7 grams
• A typical protein bar	20–30 grams

EAT CARBOHYDRATES TOWARDS THE MORE COMPLEX END OF THE SCALE

Rye bread instead of white bread, for example. In my opinion carbohydrate intake should constitute approximately 60 per cent of the total calories for the day.

So this means that if you consume 2000 calories per day, approximately 1200 of those calories should come from quality carbohydrate sources.

KEEP YOUR FAT INTAKE TO A MINIMUM

Less than 40 grams per day ideally. Again, requirements will depend on the individual body. Try not to add any fat to your diet, other than some occasional 'healthy' fats such as fish oils, avocado, seeds, nuts and the occasional sprinkle of olive oil, or macadamia nut oil.

We don't need to 'add' good fats to our existing diet; rather we can use good fats to replace some of the less healthy (saturated fats) in our diet. I often snack on almonds through the day as a quality source of protein and healthy fat, but be careful you don't overdo it as 10 grams of almonds yields about six grams of fat. And no, you can't substitute almonds for the salted cashews and beer nuts!

DO YOUR BEST NOT TO EAT 'OUT'

This includes no take away for the first six weeks of your transition period, including lunch – take your own.

If you can't avoid eating out, generally avoid the pasta (as it's usually swimming in oil) and go for the protein source (chicken, fish, beef, etc.) with a salad or steamed vegetables. Make sure that the portion size is towards the smaller end of the scale rather than toward the professional bodybuilder end of the scale. By the way, when the waiter says something like 'the vegetarian lasagne is fantastic, there's absolutely no fat in it', don't believe him. The truth is that many people have no idea what a healthy meal is and they don't really care about your body-fat issue or your cholesterol.

NO ALCOHOL FOR THE FIRST FOUR WEEKS AT LEAST

After that, a maximum of four glasses per week.

Despite a certain amount of anecdotal evidence, alcohol is actually not one of the macro-nutrients essential for the survival of the species! Although some people seem unable to live without it, there have been several cases of people living alcohol-free for years at a time; crazy, I know.

Unfortunately we live in a society which tells us that if we don't drink we're not normal and we're missing out. It is okay to incorporate some sensible drinking into our lifestyle but it's not okay to abuse it as many people do; Monday to Thursday – no alcohol, Friday night – 27 pots.

So what's an acceptable amount?

The answer to that question will be different for different people. For example, three glasses of wine will probably have a different physiological effect on a female weighing 50 kilograms compared to a guy weighing 110 kilograms.

Most 'health' organisations suggest that a glass a day of alcohol is acceptable.

I personally recommend that people drink no more than two or three days per week and no more than two glasses at a time. If the idea of eliminating alcohol from your daily routine makes you uncomfortable or anxious then maybe it's time to do it (for a while, anyway).

STOP EATING FOUR HOURS BEFORE YOU GO TO BED

Despite what your Mum tells you, going to bed with a full stomach is actually <u>not</u> a good thing. If you are a shift worker (for example) this may be a little impractical for you.

EAT TWO TO FOUR PIECES OF FRUIT PER DAY

This doesn't mean four grapes either! Fruit can constitute an entire meal. For example, I often eat nothing but fruit before lunch time. I might eat two or three pieces at breakfast and then the same mid-morning, which means by lunch I have eaten five or six pieces of fruit. I don't suggest existing on a fruit only diet as our body needs other macro-nutrients (fat, protein) but having meals which are 'fruit only' in your diet is perfectly fine. It's a great way to get some quality fibre, some quality vitamins and minerals and a good way to stay hydrated.

INCLUDE VEGETABLES (COOKED OR RAW) IN AT LEAST TWO OF YOUR MEALS

DRINK AT LEAST TWO LITRES OF WATER PER DAY

Water requirements vary greatly depending on body size, activity level and environmental temperature – many people are regularly dehydrated and don't know it. I drink about four litres of water each day.

DRINK A MAXIMUM OF THREE CUPS OF COFFEE OR TEA PER DAY (NONE IS BETTER)

Keep the cappuccino intake to an absolute minimum; you probably don't need all the extra milk or calories. Most herbal teas are fine.

NO CHEESE FOR THE FIRST SIX WEEKS (MAYBE A LITTLE LOW-FAT COTTAGE IF YOU ARE DESPERATE!)

Then minimal after that – most cheese is very high in fat – choose the lower fat options. The one kilo slab of the 'vintage tasty' in the fridge is a scary sight.

NO LOLLIES, CAKES OR SWEET BISCUITS FOR THE FIRST SIX WEEKS – PREFERABLY FOREVER!

Most sweet biscuits are very high in sugar, low in fibre, low in nutritional value and quite often high in fat. If you *need* a biscuit, try something like an Arnott's Vita-Weat Crispbread (high in fibre, low in fat and sugar) with some sugarless jam (available at any supermarket). Lollies destroy your teeth and mess with your blood-sugar and your insulin production.

PREFERABLY LOW-FAT DAIRY ONLY

PLAN YOUR MEALS FOR THE DAY EACH MORNING

Especially if you have a busy lifestyle. This doesn't mean that you are obsessed; it means you are organised and responsible.

Don't let yourself get into a situation where you are out and you find yourself consumed by hunger (as I often do) with no access to quality food. The old 'it was the best thing I could find' excuse doesn't work any more.

KNOW WHAT YOU'RE PUTTING INTO YOUR BODY

A few years ago my father was diagnosed with type-two diabetes. He had a chat to the doctor who advised him that he needed to make some significant changes to his diet.

So, armed with a new outlook, a little education and a new level of motivation, he and my mother headed off to the supermarket. The following weekend I went bush to stay with my parents for a couple of days.

Not long after I arrived the conversation turned to my father's health and he proudly informed me that he was now eating cereal for breakfast (a significant breakthrough for a bacon and eggs man).

He told me that the new breakfast menu was 97 per cent fat-free. I told him that was fantastic and asked if I could look at which cereal he was eating. He confidently strode to the pantry and handed me the box with *'97% fat-free'* emblazoned across the front.

When I read the nutritional information label and informed him that his super cereal was actually about 33 per cent sugar, he was devastated.

Isn't it amazing that the box did not have 'one-third of this stuff is actually sugar' plastered across the front? I guess they might not sell as much!

You mean they don't really care about our health?

They just want to sell products? Weird.

One of my friends is a part-time actor who does a few TV ads from time-to-time. Recently she has been splashed across the screen advertising a new super-duper weight-loss drink in powder form. The drink is mixed up by the user.

I was giving her a hard time (the ad is a bit cheesy) and asked what the stuff actually tasted like. I won't tell you what her answer was, but she did say that she would bring me a few sachets to try, as they had provided her with enough product for the next millennium.

The next time I saw her she handed me a few sachets and as usual I went straight to the nutritional information to discover that while it was only one per cent fat, it was 57 per cent sugar. Compare this 'weight loss' product with my personal favourite chocolate bar, the 'Kit Kat', which checks in at about 44 per cent sugar.

So, what's the point?

The point is to learn to read food labels and know exactly what you are putting in your mouth.

These companies are not interested in your health or well-being. They are interested in selling as many products as possible.

If you go to a restaurant and order a meal and they tell you it has 'no fat', don't believe them. Unless you have ordered a salad with no dressing you should assume that most meals in most restaurants will have at least a moderate amount of fat.

The only way you can know for sure what is in your cooked meal is if you prepare it yourself. Many times I have ordered meals which I have been informed have no added fat (butter, oil).

The food arrives at my table and I don't even need to taste it as I can see that it is swimming in oil. Don't be paranoid about eating out but don't be naïve and assume the vegetable lasagne is a good option because it has vegies in it!

It amazes me that some of us spend countless hours and dollars ensuring that our car looks great and performs optimally, but when it comes to our body it often seems that close enough is good enough. We'll only use the premium fuel for our car but with our own health it seems that the low-octane choice will suffice – 'it's cereal, surely that must be a healthy breakfast?'

Every day Australians make terrible decisions when it comes to their food intake; decisions which could be life enhancing actually become detrimental to their health and well being. Quite often it's simply a matter of educating ourselves when it comes to analysing the ingredients of products and learning to read, and taking advantage of the nutritional information labels which are now compulsory on virtually all food products.

Most nutritional labels will provide all the information you need; that is, tell you how much protein, fat, carbohydrate, fibre, sodium, cholesterol, vitamins, minerals and energy (calories) are in the product. When you look at the nutritional label you will usually find that on the right hand side the contents are broken down into 'contents per 100 grams', so you can easily see how much protein, fat (etc.) each 100 grams of a particular food contains. If you're near your pantry now go and grab a product and have a practise; it's easy stuff. Always read the 'per 100 grams' column as the 'per serving' column can be misleading as serving sizes vary greatly from product to product and company to company. Don't assume that because something has terms like 'lite' or 'reduced fat' on them that they are actually the best available product or the best choice for you. I've already outlined guidelines for macro-nutrient (fat, protein and carbohydrates) consumption earlier on, so now that you know how to read labels you can put your new-found knowledge to work.

TOO MUCH FOOD!

As simple and as obvious as it may seem to say that we eat too much, the reality is that a huge percentage of us consistently eat more food than we need every single day and, sometimes, every single meal.

We don't know when to stop. Sometimes we are so out of control that we will eat until we feel sick. If the average overeating Australian did nothing to their diet other than reduce their food intake by 10 to 40 per cent, they would probably feel better, look better and function better in a relatively short amount of time.

I am not suggesting you decrease your intake by 40 per cent tomorrow but I am suggesting that for many people merely reducing their daily intake (consistently, not just for a week) is enough to create the change they seek.

Sometimes I say to my clients, 'don't change what types of food you eat, just eat 30 per cent less.' Invariably bodies will begin to change in the first week.

It is not that they necessarily eat bad food, it is just that they eat too much based on their body's needs. What we are accustomed to eating is not necessarily an indication of what we need in terms of energy requirements.

When you have been over-eating for years, it can be difficult to discern genuine hunger because you are so used to eating whenever you have the slightest craving or the slightest stimulation.

For example, sometimes all it takes is the sight or smell of food for us to think we are experiencing hunger (when one minute before we were not the least bit hungry).

I would hate to think how many times I have walked past a rather well-known fast food outlet, been embraced by that special aroma and then suddenly realised that I need (not want) some fries and a burger, right now!

I am currently consulting a guy who has decreased his food intake by 40 per cent (he was eating way too much). Interestingly we did not actually change the type of food he ate but merely the amount. He eats the same meals, just smaller in size and as I write this, the weight is falling off him. Apart from the fact that it is healthier for him, it is also cheaper! He can take 40 per cent off his grocery bill – there's a bonus.

Sometimes we need to forget the high protein, low carbohydrate, low glycemic-index, good fats, bad fats, blah, blah, blah diet debate and just eat less. You do need some fat, protein, carbohydrates, vitamins and minerals but the average Australian diet more than covers those needs, so don't get too paranoid or concerned. The chances of you getting sick from over-indulging and being obese are significantly higher than they are of you getting sick from under-eating or being malnourished.

So, put your diet books away and just eat less. My recommendation to you is five or six small (that means small) meals per day. This means that your mid-morning snack and your dinner are both about the same size – messes with your head, doesn't it?

You also need to re-define what you consider to be a 'meal'. A meal might be a piece of fruit or a low-fat yoghurt or a protein shake. It doesn't have to be served on a plate or at a table to meet your nutritional needs.

That's one of those 'beliefs' that we talked about earlier that we need to change. Many of us have a belief and an expectation that dinner should be bigger than our mid-afternoon snack (that is why we call a 'snack' a snack after all) and that certain meals should be huge and others small.

As a general rule, five or six small meals per day is much better for our digestive system, energy levels, sporting performance and waist line than the traditional Australian custom of a cigarette and coffee for breakfast followed by a small to medium-sized farm animal and a slab for lunch.

I have yet to find any research that says that at different times of the day our bodies need drastically different-sized meals – yet this is typically how we eat.

Research and experience shows that our body functions best having small frequent meals all roughly the same size. I am talking about what is best for your body, in terms of you achieving your goals and maintaining health, not what you prefer or what you are accustomed to.

If you get to a point later in the day where you are ravenously out of control with hunger, then you have under-eaten through the day. You will adapt.

Many people are starving at night because they eat next to nothing all day. So, bottom line – keep all of your meals small and roughly the same size – even if it bothers some people or it is not the standard. If it's a bit inconvenient, get more organised. What would you prefer: to be inconvenienced or to be fat and unhealthy?

NOT ENOUGH FOOD

Like over-eating, under-eating is also an unhealthy habit. Our body needs a certain amount of micro and macro-nutrients to function optimally and when we starve ourselves all we do is put our health at risk.

Unfortunately there are many people who alternate between over-eating and under-eating. These behaviours are typically associated with people who have eating disorders but the reality is there are a great number of people who might not technically be classified as having an eating disorder yet are constantly bingeing and starving. They over-eat and then eat nothing to compensate.

When we under-eat we slow our metabolism (the rate at which

our body uses fuel), lose muscle mass, lose fluid and put our body in a state of distress.

Invariably when people who have been starving themselves go back to eating 'normally' their bodies will over-compensate, pile on the weight and their 'new' slow metabolism will make it even harder for them to create their perfect body.

Remember, anything extreme is not going to work long term.

I am constantly talking to people who believe that if they eat way less they will get 'skinnier' faster. What they are often doing in reality is losing muscle and retaining (or even increasing) bodyfat.

Quite often your body will rid itself of muscle before it will shed any fat. So what we end up with are these fat/skinny bodies.

I evaluated a new client (female, 160 centimetres, 51 kilograms) who looked somewhat thin(ish) in clothes yet when I measured her body fat it was over 30 per cent (not ideal) and out of street clothes she was actually quite flabby.

When I investigated her diet I discovered she only ever ate two meals per day. On performing a basic strength test, her results reflected the type of results I would expect for a 70-year-old woman (she is 31). The reason she is so light is that she has very little muscle for someone her age and she under-eats. Don't assume that a light body equals a good body or a lean body.

Don't under-eat.

TOO MUCH FOOD, TOO LATE IN THE DAY

Many of us eat our biggest meal at a time when we are heading into the least active phase of our day. In terms of activity, what do we typically do after we have eaten dinner?

For many people the post-dinner ritual is comprised of two to four hours of sitting, followed by six to 10 hours of lying down; both big calorie burners!

We don't need a big meal at any time of the day, especially just before we go to bed. As I said earlier, don't confuse 'habitual eating' with what your body needs. Many of us are socially programmed to eat a lot late at night just because that is what we have always done.

I recently went to a 40th birthday (for an older friend). The dinner booking was for 7.30pm and it was a set menu. There were seven courses with the first course being served at 8pm and the last course served just after 11pm!

Unfortunately this is pretty standard behaviour in one of the fattest countries in the world. Apart from the obscene amount of food that was consumed over a three-hour period, people were eating until nearly midnight. Amazingly, I was the only person who thought that eating for three and a half hours might have been a little excessive.

BREAKFAST

Not eating breakfast is a common mistake made by many people trying to lose weight. The longer we go without eating the more we slow down our metabolism. The slower our metabolism is, the more likely we are to store fat rather than burn fat.

People often say to me that they are not particularly hungry at breakfast time. Invariably these people either eat a big dinner or a late dinner, or both.

If you don't feel hungry at breakfast time then eat a small healthy dinner early in the evening and then eat nothing at all afterwards. This should cure you – you will be hungry the following morning!

If you have struggled to consistently eat a proper breakfast, try to abstain from eating for a minimum of four hours before bed. So, if you are going to bed at 11pm, stop eating (completely) at 7pm. If you get to bed at midnight, don't eat past 8pm. This is a suggestion only but it seems to work well for many of my clients.

FOOD FIBS

A few years ago I trained a woman who, like many of my clients, was desperate to lose weight. She came to me after doing the rounds of various establishments and after trying a range of programs and products, all with very little success.

As we spoke about her nutritional habits for the first time, I sensed that she was telling me one lie after another. The likelihood of her weighing 120-plus kilograms and existing on the diet that she described to me seemed very unlikely.

When I told her that I found it hard to believe that she ate so little, she was (apparently) offended. As politely as I could, I said that based on what I knew about nutrition and physiology it was pretty much impossible to eat what she claimed to be eating, and maintain the bodyweight she did.

The quick version of this story is that the initial 15-minute chat turned into a two-hour therapy session complete with tears and tissues. After about an hour she admitted to me that she binged constantly but was too embarrassed and ashamed to admit it to herself or anyone else.

This bingeing included car trips in the middle of the night to buy chocolate and ice-cream (all without the knowledge of her family) and mid-afternoon binges when she had the house to herself.

As soon as we got everything out into the open and addressed the real issues (got honest) she began to make genuine progress and create positive change. Sometimes there are issues which need to be addressed before we can even get down to the practical concerns of eating and exercise habits: issues such as living in some 'parallel universe' when it comes to honest self-assessment about habits and behaviours.

Many of us lie about our eating behaviours on at least a semi-regular basis. I have lied to myself and to others at various times over the years. I remember 10 years ago weighing 117 kilograms, eating everything that wasn't nailed down and telling people that I never ate rubbish.

That was only because I convinced myself that a hamburger with the lot was the complete nutritional package and because I didn't want to look like I was out of control with my eating, when that is exactly what I was; out of control.

I talk to people who swear black and blue that they are eating 'perfectly' and week after week they gain weight – quite an effort when you are eating perfectly.

We lie for all sorts of reasons but in order for us to create genuine long-term change we need to be up front with everything, otherwise we are just kidding ourselves.

Don't think that food issues are solely the domain of 'Mr and Mrs Average'. I have worked with personal trainers, doctors and dieticians who have eating disorders. When I want to find out what someone really eats, I ask their partner. When I have a guy who is not losing weight and something does not seem to make sense (based on the information he is giving me), I ask his wife or girlfriend about his dietary habits. Invariably her version of what goes into his mouth is way different from the story he is telling.

The times in my life when I have gained significant weight have always been because I have eaten badly. That is it – no excuses, no long-winded explanations: just unhealthy eating and bad behaviours.

Honesty. See, it's easy.

I estimate that more than half of my clients lie or have lied to me about their eating habits. Don't beat yourself up, but do be realistic, objective and honest about your eating habits.

I spoke to a lady recently who swore to me that she only ate two meals a day but couldn't lose weight. When I investigated her lifestyle (she is Italian), I discovered that she has seven children and spends all day preparing meals for her seven kids and her husband.

What she was doing was picking at food all day. From 7am until

10pm she would be eating bits and pieces of whatever she was preparing. She didn't eat twice a day; she ate 30 times a day.

Sure, she only had two 'set' meals but she was putting food in her mouth constantly. She was deluding herself.

Sometimes when I take this road in my seminars I get accused of being a little hardcore. I don't mean to be offensive or insensitive but I am adamant and passionate about being totally honest and responsible about what we put in our mouth.

Many people delude themselves about their diet. We tell ourselves we have a 'pretty good diet' when in reality we eat badly. We try and convince ourselves that we have a 'relatively healthy lifestyle' when in reality we are slowly killing ourselves with bad habits (eating and exercise).

As long as we don't display any major symptoms or signs of sickness we figure we must be 'pretty healthy'.

Many people who are on an endless mission to find 'the answer' are wasting their time because it's not only about the diet, the program or the gym, it's about getting into reality, toughening up a bit and being totally honest about what we do to our bodies.

If you had spent as much time as I have with people who constantly tell lies about their eating habits, you would understand why I believe that honesty is crucial if we are to make real progress and create genuine change.

EMOTIONAL EATING

Too many of us eat for comfort rather than because we are genuinely hungry.

Food can be very soothing and therapeutic; it can also be the cause of depression, anxiety and emotional distress. For many people food is the drug of choice when it comes to medicating depression or emotional stress.

If you have historically been an emotional eater then you

need to create a plan to combat those emotional eating urges. You can't just wish them away, there must be a strategy or the behaviour will continue.

It is impossible for me to tell you here what your specific plan and course of action should be, but knowing what your stumbling blocks are will help.

Identifying what you do and how and why you do it are the first steps. Beyond that it is up to you to create some new rules and boundaries for yourself. It is also crucial for you to have the discipline and determination to implement your new rules and plan.

For example, if you know that you usually overeat when you are depressed, make a rule that next time you feel like a 'depression binge', you will do some exercise instead.

Considering the fact that exercise is one of the best anti-depressants available this isn't a bad idea. Imagine the effect on your body and your attitude if you did a five or 10-kilometre run instead of eating a tub of ice-cream every time you were depressed.

Emotional eating will only add to the problem rather than fix it; it might be an enjoyable temporary distraction but it is never going to be a long-term solution.

PICKING

Some people take the 'grazing' concept a little out of context. If you are making the kids' lunches and you lick the knife, eat a crust or chew on half a biscuit then you are shovelling calories into your body, calories that your body must do something with. Eating is eating. I am sure some people believe that if they eat while standing up the calories don't count. If you are serious about dropping some weight and bodyfat then do not eat outside of your set meals … at all.

This might seem hardcore but it works. Most of us need clearly defined parameters and it is my experience that people who have a history of weight problems get the best results when their meals are a clearly defined event, rather than a continual blurry haze of eating.

If you have the lolly jar at home or on the desk at work, get rid of it. Don't pick.

TOO MUCH PROCESSED FOOD AND TOO LITTLE FIBRE

Every second person I meet is constipated on at least a semi-regular basis. This is often because they have a diet high in processed foods and low in dietary fibre.

When we increase the fibre and decrease the processed junk we usually see an improvement in bowel health. As a general rule, the more processed the food, the less there is in it for you in terms of quality nutrition.

Depending on how much you weigh and which guidelines you follow, it is suggested that the average adult needs around 40 to 50 grams of fibre per day (as mentioned earlier in my nutritional guidelines) – in my experience this seems to be about right.

To give you more of an idea of what this means; an apple with skin contains about four grams of fibre, a slice of white bread has about 0.6 grams, a slice of dark rye bread about three grams and most cereals are somewhere in the one to five grams of fibre per 100 grams of cereal range.

For example, Special K (according to the label on the box) contains 2.5 grams of fibre for every 100 grams of cereal. So if you wanted to meet all your fibre needs through Special K you would need to consume about two kilograms of it per day!

Even 100 grams of raw rolled oats (which you might think would be very high in fibre) only contains about 10 grams of fibre.

BE ORGANISED, PLAN WELL, MAKE GOOD CHOICES

As with any worthwhile endeavour, eating properly requires forward thinking, organisation and planning, especially when you have a busy lifestyle.

Some people gain weight because they always eat on the run and choose from whatever is available at the time.

Some people just don't plan ahead. A client thought he was eating well because he chose the 'healthy options' at work for lunch. The truth is he was too lazy to make his own lunch and get organised.

In his words his healthy lunch consisted of:

> One chicken and salad roll;
> a healthy low-fat 'bar thing'; and
> a skim milk cappuccino.

One day I met him at his work to discuss a seminar I was doing for his company and as it was lunch-time, we decided to talk business and eat at the same time. He ordered his 'usual' (which was how he ordered it) and I ordered a chicken salad.

When his 'usual' came I was astounded at how unhealthy his 'healthy' lunch was. His chicken and salad roll was actually chicken schnitzel, cheese, mayonnaise, butter and a token green on a white bread roll.

The 'healthy low-fat bar thing' was actually a high-fat, high-sugar muesli bar and his skinny cappuccino was a mug of coffee, with reduced-fat (not skim) milk.

I estimated the nutritional breakdown of his lunch to be:

Roll	50 grams of fat, 700 calories
'Health' bar	22 grams of fat, 320 calories (from the label)
Coffee	4 grams of fat, 150 calories
Total calories	**1170**
Total fat	**76 grams**

This lunch had more fat than he should consume in a whole day (the recommended daily intake is about 40 grams) as well as about half his daily calorie requirements.

Just to put it in perspective, a Big Mac has 24 grams of fat and 500 calories. Here is a guy who would spend $200 per week on personal training to change his body yet not spend 10 minutes in the morning planning and organising his food for the day.

If you are not certain that you can access the type of food you should be eating through the day then make your own and take it to work or school, have some healthy emergency snacks (like yoghurt or fruit) or re-educate whoever it is who provides your lunch!

If I order a chicken and salad sandwich and it comes out with anything that I didn't ask for, I send it back. Remember, you need to be serious about getting results; don't accept anything less than you require. By the way, my chicken salad contained about five to six grams of fat and between 400-500 calories.

IN SUMMARY

- More small meals, fewer formal meal times.
- Eat less, but don't 'under-eat'.
- Finish your last meal three to four hours before bed-time.
- Be honest with yourself.
- Know what you're eating – check the labels.
- Know what you're eating – cook it yourself.
- Avoid emotional eating.
- Don't eat outside of your set meals (don't pick).
- Remember, more natural foods, less processed foods.
- When you change your eating habits, do it gradually.
- When in doubt, avoid or take your own.
- Don't miss breakfast.
- Check your fibre intake.

CHAPTER 10

HOW TO EXERCISE WELL

There's no program for everyone, but there is one set of rules that form a framework for all.

I don't personally advocate any particular system of training as I believe that there is no single approach to exercise which is appropriate for every body.

In fact, one of my pet hates is when people go to a gym and they are put on a generic program. 'Just warm up on the bike and then complete exercises one to 10 on the wall charts'. When you have two people with different needs, goals and body types both following the same program, it is little wonder that they get frustrated and disappointed with their lack of results. This happens every day in gyms throughout the world.

While getting in shape is not always easy and will invariably involve a degree of discipline, commitment and mental toughness, many people do their best to make the process more technical and more difficult than it needs to be.

If we stick with certain common sense principles then we can consistently produce outstanding results with far less fuss than most of the 'experts' would have you believe.

Having a degree in Exercise Science and 20 years of experience watching people do all sorts of strange things to their bodies, I thought it would be negligent of me not to at least discuss some of the most common issues and challenges that we need to negotiate as we create our perfect body. Here they are:

1. Find the program which is right for you.
This might mean spending a few dollars and enlisting the services of a professional in order to develop an approach which is specific to your needs. If five readers of this book came to me, I would prescribe five different workout and diet plans; two would be similar, one would be unique and the other two would have a core of similarities but significant other differences. Following the wrong program, even with a good attitude and a strong commitment, will usually prove to be an exercise in frustration. So it is imperative that you do what's appropriate for your physiology and goals. Here are some examples of programs for different people.

EXERCISE GUIDELINES AND RECOMMENDATIONS
These are guidelines only for someone who does not currently have a high level of fitness and would probably rate themselves at the beginner end of the scale.

I have added these guidelines just to give you an idea of where you might start when it comes to your exercise — this is not a personalised program.

If you have not exercised for a long time, if you are not particularly fit or if you have a pre-existing medical condition make sure you see your doctor before you commence your new regime.

THE VERY UNFIT GROUP (could fall over at any time group)

- 10-20 minutes of very low intensity cardio-vascular (CV) exercise, three to five days per week (building up as you go). Include: walking, riding a stationary bike, swimming.
- Don't do the exact same exercise two days in a row if possible (this might mean that you just vary the speed or the distance of your walk).
- Sit ups and back extensions: three by 10 times per day.
- Stretch: 10 minutes every day
- Light weight training (if possible and practical): 10-20 minutes, one to two times per week (supervised).
- Don't do any intense exercise (e.g. squash, tennis, hard running).
- If all you do initially is walk every day, that is a great place to start – as you get a little fitter just walk quicker or further.

THE MODERATELY UNFIT GROUP (gee my back is sore group)

- 15-30 minutes of low intensity CV exercise, four to six days per week (building up as you go). Include: walking (uphill or flat), riding a bike (indoors or outdoors), swimming, gentle exercise class (gym).
- Don't do the exact same exercise two days in a row if possible.
- Stretch: 10 minutes every day.
- Sit ups and back extensions – three by 15 times per day
- Light weight training if possible and practical; 15-30 minutes, one to two times per week (supervised initially).
- Very social, leisurely tennis game would be okay but ease into it.

THE SLIGHTLY UNFIT GROUP (if the house was on fire I could probably make it out group)

- 20-40 minutes of low to moderate intensity CV exercise, four to six days per week (building up as you go). Include: walking (uphill or flat), walking/jogging (increase the amount of jogging as your fitness increases), riding a bike (indoors or outdoors), swimming, gentle exercise class (gym), CV machines at the gym at a low level (stepper, rower, strider, treadmill, grinder).
- Don't do the exact same exercise two days in a row if possible.
- Sit ups and back extensions: three by 20 times per day.
- Light weight training if possible and practical. 20-40 minutes, two times per week (supervised initially).
- Stretch: 10 minutes every day.

Remember the above guidelines are just that; guidelines – not a personalised program. If you've identified what group you might fit into all you need to do is start moving those limbs and get going. Start slowly, ease into it and remember something is better than nothing. If all you can do on day one is walk 100 metres, then walk 100 metres - by day 30 you will probably be walking a kilometre! Some people are so disheartened by their sorry shape that they never actually start because the task seems insurmountable. No matter which program you follow it needs to be progressive over time, so where we start doesn't really matter as much as where we end up. Don't focus on what you can't do, focus on what you can do and start there. If three step-ups is your maximum, then do three today and do four tomorrow or the day after. Make sure that no matter which program you follow, you progress your exercise regime slowly and intelligently over the initial few months; walk further or quicker, lift more (weight or repetitions), stretch further or move from a walk to a gentle jog.

2. Stick at it – be consistent.

If you are at the point where you are genuinely ready to change, make consistency of effort your priority when it comes to your exercise program.

Remember, the number one reason why people don't achieve their goals is that they don't finish what they start – so, finish what you start. Don't be one of those people who is forever making decisions that aren't followed through.

3. There are two types of training: maintenance training and progressive training.

Most people are following a maintenance program, and don't know it. For most of them, their body won't change because it doesn't need to.

If you are partial to a certain type of workout and exercise for you is merely an enjoyment thing, then that is great. But if your goal is to improve your fitness or change your body in some way, then you need to change some of the exercise variables in order to create a need for adaptation. We need to give our body a reason to get leaner, lighter or stronger; a reason to change.

Many people who exercise regularly are simply going through the motions. For some people going to the gym is more of a social outing than anything else.

They are consistently turning up and doing the same thing they did yesterday and last week, same weights, same reps, same bike, same treadmill, same intensity, same everything. You need to give your body a reason to change. If you continually do the same thing, the same way, your body will continually look the same.

The process of getting fitter, stronger, leaner, bigger or smaller is one of physiological adaptation. When you lift weights and your muscles grow, this is your body responding to physical stress. When you run the same course and each week it gets progressively easier, this is an indication that your body is adapting to the stress you are putting on it.

The problem is that after a while unless there is some type of change, either an increase in intensity or duration or a change in the type of exercise you are doing, the progress will come to a grinding halt.

If, for example, your thing is running, then maybe you can keep running, but perhaps you need to change how you run.

If you have been running on the flat, incorporate some hills into your program or maybe run some stairs. That will sort you out.

If you have been running on a hard surface, then incorporate some soft sand running; a world of pain. Not only is sand effective in terms of improving fitness, but you will also use about twice the energy (calories) as running on a hard surface for the same amount of time.

Maybe you've been plodding 10 kilometres at six-minute (per kilometre) pace, so go out and run half the distance at a much quicker pace. Get my point? Change the intensity, the duration and the structure and your body will change because it needs to and because it is being stimulated in a different way.

If we generally do the same thing, the same way, we tend to develop a limited type of fitness. We become fit for what we do. If all we do is swim, we develop swimming fitness.

Yes, we do improve overall fitness but not to the same level as if we were to cross-train (do different types of exercise). Take a swimmer for a run up a few hills and see how fit they are.

When we do the same type of exercise all the time we are:

- More likely to get injured because we are constantly stressing the same muscles and joints the same way.
- Less likely to change because we don't give our body a reason to do so.
- More likely to lose motivation because what we do is repetitious and monotonous.

If you walk a lot you become fit for walking. If you lift weights all the time you become fit for pumping iron. If you want a higher level of fitness, less injuries, a more balanced type of fitness and faster overall results, keep your exercise program varied.

If, hypothetically, you have made a decision to do five, 30-minute sessions of cardio per week, I would suggest you do (for example) a swim, a bike ride, a run, some boxing and a stair session rather than doing five sessions on the bike, or five sessions of any one activity.

If you have been doing the same thing, the same way, change it from today. As you know by now, today is the right day.

About six years ago I met Tammy Van Wisse who is a very accomplished international marathon swimmer. We got talking and she decided that she would start some training with me to break up her existing program, which revolved largely around swimming.

The first day I trained Tammy I decided we would do an easy warm-up jog followed by some varied cardiovascular work and a few weights; essentially something different from what she was used to.

At the start of the session we headed out the front door of the gym to do a one-kilometre easy, slow(ish) warm-up jog. By the time we got back to the gym I had a world champion marathon swimmer who was nearly dead from a little jog!

Here was this athlete who would regularly swim 10 kilometres before most of us are out of bed, struggling to complete a basic short run. Why? She was an incredibly efficient swimming (not running) machine because her body had specifically adapted to the type of training it was subjected to – swimming.

Incidentally, it is not crucial, or even desirable, for marathon swimmers to have low bodyfat, so the marathon swimmer who trains in an environment where her bodyweight is supported found pounding the pavement, in a marathon swimmer's body, quite a challenge.

As soon as Tammy introduced some variety into her program her overall fitness improved straight away.

4. Don't do what you're good at, do what works.

In one of my gyms I have three steppers, which are hard work to say the least, but they are a fantastic workout and they burn a gazillion calories per hour. Next to these steppers are four bikes which are super comfortable, require less effort and are relatively easy to use. Guess which machines don't get used?

If you have two exercise options and one is harder for you than the other, the harder option is the one which will probably give you the most benefit in terms of creating change and causing your body to adapt. Bummer.

Sorry … I didn't make it that way; it's just how it works.

5. Training records

A food and training diary is one of the most effective ways to increase your chances of achieving your goals.

Keeping a record of your dietary and exercise habits is a great way to make the 'getting in shape' process a methodical and productive one and provides us with the following benefits:

i. **Organisation:** Having to record your exercise habits and food intake usually means that you will be more organised in terms of planning and structuring your meals and your exercise.

For many people, diarising everything makes the whole process of getting in shape a lot more structured and logical rather than a hit or miss adventure.

ii. **Awareness:** When we record everything that goes into our mouth, honestly and accurately, and every minute of exercise, it is usually a big eye-opener.

Record every single thing in a detailed manner, not so you become obsessed but so that you have a realistic picture of what you do to your body over time.

Many people have come to me after filling in a diary for a while and told me how shocked they were when they analysed what they do to their bodies over the course of a week or a month. Too many people kid themselves about their eating and exercise habits.

iii. **Discipline:** For many people keeping a record of everything means that they are less likely to 'lose the plot'. Many of my clients tell me that the diary helps them stay disciplined and focused.

Sometimes I am scared to mention the 'D' word because some people equate discipline to a life of misery and deprivation. I personally believe that discipline is an absolute necessity if we want to create success in any area of our lives.

Without the discipline to consistently follow through on the decisions we make we will consistently end up back where we started or worse.

iv. **Motivation:** A diary can be a great motivational tool as we can objectively gauge our progress as we go, by recording all of our training on a daily basis. It is a great motivator to be able to flick back through the months and to see the improvements we have made.

v. **Education:** By recording our food and our training and by monitoring results we can learn what works for us. It is important that we learn what works best for our bodies and a diary is a great way to do this. A diary also helps us identify patterns and habits that we need to factor into the process and deal with.

vi. **Feedback:** If you decide to enlist the services of a health professional like a trainer and/or a dietician, then a well-kept diary can be a tremendous asset.

When someone comes to see me and they have a diary which has been filled out accurately for the last six weeks or six months, it makes my job much easier. All I have to do is read what they have been doing, interpret it and advise them.

IN SUMMARY

- Some exercise is better than no exercise.
- Find the best program for you – different bodies need a different approach.
- Consistency is crucial.
- Your body won't change if you don't give it a reason to.
- Don't only do what you enjoy, do what works.
- Keep a record of your training – it will help you figure out what works for you.

SECTION THREE

COMMON FAILINGS AND HOW TO BEAT THEM

You might struggle along the way; it's how you cope with those challenges that will separate you from the pack.

Chapter 11 **Falling off the wagon** 110
It happens to most ... jump back on

Chapter 12 **Finish what you start** 113
Don't be half-hearted. Complete the job

Chapter 13 **The time factor** 120
You have the time ... get organised

Chapter 14 **The fine line between discipline and obsession** 126
Recognise the difference

Chapter 15 **It's about you, not your 'mates'** 130
Don't expect universal support. It's up to you

Chapter 16 **Social eating** 134
Learn the art of eating out

Chapter 17 **Don't confuse the six-pack with inner peace** 139
They are not the same

Chapter 18 **Don't be a spoilsport** 141
Enjoy the fruits of your labour

CHAPTER 11

FALLING OFF THE WAGON

It's normal to stumble occasionally on the long journey. Deal with it and move on.

If you are like most people then at some stage along the way you are going to have hiccups. Before you throw yourself off the top step, do your best to take the emotion out of the situation and realise that the most dangerous thing about 'falling off the wagon' and shovelling some chips or chocolate down the hatch from time to time, is not so much the unnecessary calories, but more the psychological reaction that often follows those unnecessary calories.

How you react after you have a slip-up along the way is crucial to your long-term success. If every time you make a mistake you throw in the towel and start beating yourself up (as some people do), then you will never create your best body.

There may be times when, for whatever reason, you eat something or do something which is not consistent with what you are trying to achieve. You might not train or exercise for a day, or a week or you might 'accidentally' eat a kilo of rocky-road (as many of my clients do).

Everybody does this and it is not the end of the world. It is actually an opportunity for you to learn a little bit about yourself. For some people a night of bad eating or a few days without exercise will spell the beginning of the end. 'What's the point?' many people will say. 'I've stuffed it up now – I may as well eat the whole packet!'

I have seen many people lose the plot emotionally and psychologically because they have had a moment of weakness. Some people will waste three months of hard work because they ate three chocolates and they have decided that 'it's all over'. It's not all over unless you decide it is.

Talk about an over-reaction. If you make a mistake or if you just do something stupid (as we all do), deal with it and move on. When you are trying to create your perfect body, eating a little junk from time to time can be more harmful for your mental state than for your body.

The issue is not eating the three chocolates; a few chocolates won't kill you or undo months of hard work. The real issue is the psychological damage that can happen when people 'fall off the wagon' at a time when they are mentally and emotionally fragile and their new found behaviours are not yet habits.

It's okay to make mistakes along the way; in fact it's pretty normal.

It's not okay to give up because you had a bad night, weekend or week.

If you really want to create the type of forever change that I have been prescribing, then you need to be able to deal with the challenges along the way. This is just another one.

How we eat and exercise are important considerations in the whole process but whether someone follows program A, B or C will be of no consequence if they never follow any program long enough to achieve their goals or to create habits.

Whether your preferred choice of exercise is pump classes,

mountain biking, swimming, aerobics or running is not the issue, as they all have their benefits and they all burn calories and all create change; the issue is whether or not you are still exercising consistently six, 12 or 24 months after you have made that initial decision.

If you make a decision to exercise three times a week, then exercise three times a week, every week. If you resolve that you are going to eat fruit every morning instead of bacon and eggs then don't do it for a week, do it every morning.

Does this mean that we can never have a day off? No, it means that, in this instance, the fruit and the three days exercise are the rule not the exception. It is about creating new habits, a new lifestyle, a new attitude and about being consistent.

IN SUMMARY

- It's okay to make mistakes along the way; in fact it's pretty normal.
- It's not okay to give up because you had a bad night, weekend or week.

CHAPTER 12

FINISH WHAT YOU START (COMMITMENT 101)

It's self-evident that there's no end to unfinished business, so don't start what you won't finish.

Imagine if I ran a seminar entitled:
UNLOCK THE SECRETS TO YOUR BEST BODY: HARD WORK, DISCIPLINE, COMMITMENT, SACRIFICE AND SWEAT.

No matter how great the information was, I would be talking to a room of empty chairs.

We don't want to hear that hard things like work, discipline and sweat are sometimes the answer. We want a pill and we want those special electrode things that stimulate your muscles while we eat chips and watch *Everybody Loves Raymond*. We want some previously unknown scientific fat-burning secret.

We want easy.

I am not saying that getting in shape needs to be some big macho process of discomfort, bravery and pain. In fact, done with the right attitude, getting in shape can be one of the most enjoyable experiences there is. What I am saying is that sometimes the situation dictates that we need to experience a level of discomfort in order to move from where we are (physically), to where we want to be.

When you have been existing on a diet which is high in fat, sugar and calories and then you change to five or six small healthy meals per day, there will be a period of physical, mental and emotional adjustment. If you have been consuming 5000 calories per day and then all of a sudden you change to 2000 you will more than likely experience hunger. Somewhere, on some level, you may feel like you are missing out. Does this mean you need 5000 calories daily? No, it means your body and your head is conditioned to eating a lot of food.

We live in a society where we over-eat so much that we find it hard to distinguish between genuine hunger and urges generated by habitual daily feeding rituals. We eat because it is time to eat not because we are hungry or our body needs food. We all have our eating rituals. You think about how you or someone close to you has their 'weird little food thing'. Every night in this country thousands of people eat huge dinners (more food than they need) and then 30 minutes later (when they have hardly begun to digest that dinner and could not possibly be genuinely hungry) they head to the pantry or fridge to get that ritual snack (chocolate, ice-cream, biscuits; occasionally all three).

Identify those unhealthy behaviours and habits in yourself and determine to change – not next week or next month but today.

Why can a gym which has a council permit limiting it to 100 people in the building at any given time, sell 6000 memberships? Because most people who join a gym don't go often or don't go at all, that's why. The average gym in Australia has an 'active' membership of about 15 per cent – this means that in a centre with 6000 current members approximately 5100 of those members never even turn up! Why? Because we consistently make decisions that we don't follow through on.

Every day gyms sell memberships that people won't use. Gym

owners know that every day someone will walk through the door, pay for a membership and never come back, not even once. I was talking to a guy recently in the U.S. who oversees a large chain of gyms. He told me that about 15 per cent of people who join his clubs for a year never come back for a second workout and somewhere around 25 per cent of people don't come more than five times – and I am talking about beautiful gyms with great facilities and good staff.

So, what is the take home message?

Finish what you start.

How many times in your life have you started a new program, diet, or project and fallen off the wagon within a few weeks? If you are like most people, the answer will be 'plenty'.

The biggest mistake people make every single day is throwing in the towel and not actually giving the program a chance to work, or giving themselves a real chance to create genuine change. Sometimes it seems that we live in a society where as soon as things are not easy, comfortable or convenient we call a halt to proceedings.

There are two key rules to follow to avoid failure:

1. When the initial excitement and euphoria wears off, keep going anyway.
2. Don't start something which you cannot maintain long term.

Many of us start endeavours which we are more than likely not able to maintain in the long term. We start extreme things because we want to see dramatic results in a short time.

Extreme is not healthy, mentally or physically, and it is not something we can do for the rest of our life. Many of the popular diets currently doing the rounds are, in my opinion, extreme and inappropriate.

They are extreme because they lack balance and logic (e.g. diets with virtually no carbohydrates) and for most of us, they are not maintainable and will not create forever results.

Very, very few people can maintain 'extreme' for longer than a week or two. For this reason alone the extreme approach should be avoided. For me to tell someone who has been drinking and smoking for 30 years that they need to give up both habits by next week is, for that person, extreme advice and, most likely, not achievable.

So rather than go for the hard-core approach, the average person (which is most of us) should follow something which involves changing behaviour progressively over time. This way we are more likely to create permanent, forever change.

Here is a typical scenario that I have witnessed many times:

> A guy gets to the point where he absolutely hates his body. He has been insulted and humiliated for the millionth time about his appearance and although he does the macho thing and makes a joke of it, he is hurt.
>
> He has arrived at a point where he is desperate to change. He wants to look and feel different. He is a 40-year-old, obese, recently divorced, ex-footballer (retired 13 years earlier) and figures he can drag the Dunlop Volleys out of retirement, modify his diet and be brand new in no time.
>
> It has been nine years since he has done exercise of any description, although this is apparently a minor issue. He figures he'll start out with a lazy five-kilometre run and finish off with 100 push-ups and sit-ups to get his abs and pecs going!
>
> Miraculously he struggles through his five-kilometre plod without stopping and ignores the tightness in his chest and the tingling down his left arm.
>
> He gets back from his run and completes his 100 push-ups and sit-ups (in lots of twos and threes respectively), ruptures his left pec and tears his abdominals off the bone.
>
> The next morning he has four anti-inflammatory tablets and a black coffee (the breakfast of champions) and then

drags his battered body out for another five-kilometre slog around suburbia.

He finishes his run and then, ignoring the searing pain through his entire upper body, completes 100 agonising push-ups and sit-ups. He showers and then eats half an apple and four Corn Flakes as he feels he needs to watch his food intake.

This cycle continues for anywhere between three days and three weeks and then in a moment of complete mental, physical and emotional exhaustion and depression he decides it is all too hard and throws in the towel. He has 16 beers and a family size meat-lovers' pizza to ease the pain.

This sounds too crazy to be true, doesn't it? This story (or similar) happens many times every day around Australia. We make decisions about our exercise and our diet which are not logical, rational or maintainable long term.

If you are getting back into exercise, start something appropriate for where you are at the moment (physically and mentally) and then progress the intensity and/or duration sensibly over time. This way your body and your mind can cope with the change.

From a health perspective, it is better to stay slightly overweight than it is to be constantly putting on and losing weight like many of us do.

Every time you start and stop another program you:

1. Waste more precious time.
2. Lose more confidence and self-belief.
3. Re-enforce bad habits.
4. Decrease the chances of actually achieving that perfect body.

Here's another story:

A woman had been referred to me by one of my clients. She

came to see me so that I could assess her and prescribe a program to 'get results fast'.

In the course of the consultation I discovered that this lady had worked with seven different trainers in the past four years, been a member of more than 10 different gyms over the years and in her words, started and stopped more diets than she cared to remember.

The more I talked to this woman the more I realised that the exercise programs, eating plans and trainers were not the problem; her approach was. She didn't want to sweat, she didn't want to get uncomfortable, she didn't want to lift weights, she didn't want to stop drinking alcohol daily and she didn't want to have to change her lifestyle.

She didn't need a trainer; she needed a magician. I told her so.

I asked her if I could look at the last program she had written for her. I knew the trainer who had written the program and based on what she had told me, the program seemed to be quite acceptable.

When I asked why she was unhappy with the program, she told me that it didn't work. I asked her what she meant. She said that she didn't get the results she was after. When I asked her how long she followed the program for she looked uneasy. "I'm not sure," she said, "maybe three weeks".

It's interesting that she said 'it' (the program) didn't work when, in actual fact, it was her who wasn't prepared to do the work. When I pointed this out she was not a happy camper. Maybe I missed that lecture on tact at school, but I was telling the truth. She just didn't want to hear it.

Sometimes what we need to hear is not what we want to hear. I offend people on a daily basis, not because I want to be offensive, but because I would rather be honest in my assessment of the real issues surrounding a person's inability to lose weight.

What is the point in me writing this woman exercise program number 312, when it is not about the program? What is the point of a dietician prescribing diet number 257, when it is not about the diet?

More people than I can remember have come to me weeks or months after an initial meeting and have thanked me for giving them the reality check that they needed, even though it may not have been appreciated at the time. Some people still aren't talking to me. That's okay too.

If you have had seven trainers, joined more than 10 gyms and you are still out of shape, there is a fair chance it has, at least, something to do with your personal approach and attitude to the weight loss, exercise and food thing.

So, what is the 'take home' message?

Finish what you start.

IN SUMMARY

- Don't start what you can't finish.
- Don't be extreme, be methodical.
- When the initial excitement subsides, keep going anyway.

CHAPTER 13

THE TIME FACTOR

The No. 1 reason people give for not being in shape is time. But is it really a time issue or is it an 'us' issue?

When it comes to avoiding exercise, the good old 'time' excuse has been one of my personal favourites. I have used it many times over the years. It can get you out of a tight spot on occasion but unfortunately, it doesn't really stack up when you look at it closely.

If it really is a time thing, exactly how much time do we need to invest on a weekly basis to create a positive impact on our health, fitness level and appearance and achieve the desired changes? The answer is not as much as you would think.

Depending on which exercise guidelines you look at and which expert you listen to, the norm seems to be somewhere around 30 minutes, three or four times per week.

The official Craig Harper recommendation for beginners is 20 to 45 minutes, four times per week (depending on your starting point).

Obviously the intensity, type of exercise, frequency and duration of exercise will vary from person to person, but as a general guideline this formula works for most people.

For some people this may initially mean four gentle 30-minute walks per week and for others, something a little more strenuous.

So let's analyse the time thing.

If you exercise at the upper limit of my recommendation (four 45-minute sessions per week) then you are exercising for a total of three hours per week. There are 168 hours in a week, and if you subtract 40 hours for work and 56 for sleep, there are 72 hours left for you! So a three-hour time commitment doesn't seem too unrealistic if getting in shape is as important as we make it out to be. Three hours for exercise still leaves 69 'you hours'.

Three hours doesn't seem much at all, does it? Or maybe that's just how I look at it.

If you were to spend three hours per week exercising you would be spending over 98 per cent of your time not exercising.

That's hardly an excessive commitment if we are serious about changing.

Again, it depends on what is important to you right now. If you are genuinely serious about changing your body, you will find the time, no matter your situation.

> Recently I had a married couple come to see me because they were interested in getting in shape. I figured out early in the meeting that the wife was more enthusiastic about the idea than her husband, as is often the case (sorry lads).
>
> Before long, the husband told me that he really wanted to lose weight but 'right now' was not 'in a position' (whatever that means) to be able to devote the time necessary to do this type of endeavour any justice. 'Crap' (I thought).
>
> However, I guess it sounds better than 'I can't be bothered' or 'I'm too lazy'.

I asked him if he watched TV and before he could answer, the apple of his eye chimed in with, "He lives in front of the bloody thing every night".

I asked her how much time he spent in front of the tube each evening, knowing I might get a more accurate answer from her, and she replied "from 8-11pm every night, he sits like a walrus in his special chair".

When I pointed out that seven days times an average of three hours per day equals 21 hours of television per week, he wasn't amused.

That is a big time commitment from a guy who apparently doesn't have any time! He must reaaaaally want to watch that TV. Maybe if he had the same motivation and commitment to his health and fitness as he does for his TV watching he wouldn't be in such bad physical condition.

He started to get defensive. Not wanting to incite him, I agreed with him that it was important that someone like him had down time (Craig the diplomat).

When I suggested that he decrease his TV viewing by three hours per week and increase his exercise by three hours he didn't really have anywhere to go (given that he told me 10 minutes earlier that he really wanted to lose weight).

This way he didn't need to sacrifice any of his precious work time, which was supposedly the reason he couldn't exercise in the first place (Craig the time management guru).

According to the Australian Bureau of Statistics, the average Australian watches around 20 hours of television per week.

What is the number one excuse we give for not exercising?

Time.

It is not a time thing, it is a priority thing, an organisational thing, and an I 'can't be bothered' thing.

SHIFTING RESPONSIBILITY

So if it isn't really a time issue, why do we say it is? Why do we all say it's a 'time thing' when it is really an 'us' thing?

We all do this from time to time in different areas of our lives to take the pressure off ourselves and to make ourselves look better in the eyes of others.

This is not what we want to hear but it is true and we have all done this at some stage. We think that if it is a 'time' thing and not an 'us' thing, then we don't have to change.

We say: I don't have to make any sacrifices and I don't have to get uncomfortable because the reason I look like this is not my fault. 'I cannot control how many hours there are in a week!'

We are constantly shifting responsibility so that we don't have to change or address certain things in our lives. As long as we continue to blame other people, situations and circumstances for the state of disrepair our body (and sometimes our life) is in, we will never change because we will never take responsibility and we will never make progress.

If you genuinely want to find the time, you will find the time. It is about priorities and about you being prepared to make tough decisions and follow through.

It is about you making the time.

'Right now it's more important that I sleep than get up and go for a run'.

Remember, no one makes you stay in bed; you choose to stay in bed. If you have consistently made decisions which have taken your body to a place you don't want it to be, determine that from today you will make better decisions for your body, that you will change your behaviour and that you will stop transferring responsibility.

> I was talking to an overweight guy recently who was telling me that part of his job required him to have a minimum of three business lunches or dinners every week.

He also told me that it was considered to be rude not to drink at least a moderate amount of alcohol at these outings. He told me that these obligatory commitments were the reason that he was not in shape.

When I suggested that the reason he was out of shape was at least partly because of the bad choices he made at these functions he didn't want to know about it.

When I also suggested that next time he has a function he choose the grilled fish and the salad instead of the fisherman's basket, he looked at me like I was speaking some foreign language.

Within two minutes I knew this guy was not serious about getting in shape and changing his life. He just wanted me to tell him I understood his dilemma and it was all okay.

Well, it's not okay. If you are happy to be fat and unhealthy then do nothing, but if you say you want to change yet you are not really making any genuine effort, then don't complain about the state of your body.

There have been times when, as an adult, I have gained weight and I can assure you that the reason I got fat was not my genetics, was not the business lunches, was not my mother's cooking and was not because my busy schedule wouldn't allow me to do the things I needed to do.

It was because I ate more food than I needed to, did less exercise than I should have and because I made bad choices – end of story.

No-one made me gain weight, it was 100 per cent me. Time, genetics, age, work and lifestyle are all issues which impact on how we behave and the decisions we make, but they are not <u>the</u> reason we get out of shape.

If you get out of shape, you are the reason – not the situation or circumstances you find yourself in.

As I said before I have a body type that gains weight easily. As I write this I am 40 years old, 178(ish) centimetres, weigh 80 kilos and have eight per cent body fat.

The reason I am in good shape is not because I am genetically gifted but because I do the right things consistently for my body. I take full responsibility for the things that I do and don't do to my body.

You are always going to have obstacles and challenges which make it harder for you to get and stay in shape. That's life.

So, stop waiting for the perfect time, stop shifting responsibility, stop making excuses ... it's all up to you.

IN SUMMARY

- There's plenty of time: chart your week and you'll see the gaps for you.
- Be responsible, don't avoid the issue.
- By not making a decision, you are making a decision.
- As little as two to three hours of exercise per week can create amazing change.
- It's not about time, it's about you.

CHAPTER 14

THE FINE LINE BETWEEN DISCIPLINE AND OBSESSION

Recognise the difference.
Discipline is in control.
Obsession is out of control.

Isn't the difference between obsession and discipline merely a matter of perception and definition? To different people, different behaviours represent different things. To me drinking alcohol every day of our life is an unhealthy, irrational behaviour. To many people it is a normal and totally acceptable behaviour. For them to admit that it is unhealthy and irrational would mean that they would have to change, so therefore they will define it as acceptable – even 'normal'.

'I work hard all day, I deserve this' is a common justification or rationalisation.

I exercise most days of my life. I consider that to be a healthy behaviour and a valuable habit for me. For someone else (depending on their point of reference) they may consider daily exercise to be obsessive and unbalanced. How do we decide what is healthy and what is not? Here's how:

Disciplined people are in control.
Obsessed people are out of control.
Discipline is healthy.
Obsession is unhealthy.

When it gets to the point where you get distressed or anxious if you cannot do your daily workout (and this happens more often than you might imagine) then you are on your way to being obsessed.

This is the point when exercise shifts from being a healthy habit to an unhealthy obsession. I have seen this happen many times and it can sneak up on you without you realising it.

When someone changes their body significantly and, as a result of that change their world is a better place, then it is easy to understand how they might become paranoid about 'losing' what they have gained. They panic about losing momentum and focus, and getting fat again.

Fat represents pain and we become so determined not to regain the weight that we create a whole new list of things to worry about:

- **What if I get injured and cannot train?**
- **What if I lose motivation?**
- **What if it stops working?**

Pretty soon we start to create problems that don't exist:

- **I feel fat today.**
- **I think my backside is bigger.**
- **What if I go out and there's no healthy food to eat?**
- **What if I get up tomorrow and I am not in the zone any more?**

In no time we become obsessed with our food and exercise.

I know a woman who weighs herself up to 100 times per day.

She will weigh herself and then go to the toilet and weigh herself again two minutes later.

Although she is in quite good shape physically, her anxiety and fear about getting fat again are probably more painful and detrimental to her health than her previously chubby body was. Her problem is not her body; it is her obsessive thinking and behaviours. We must be in control of our eating and our exercise, not the other way around.

As I mentioned earlier, when I was about 14 years old and was working my way through the 'Jumbo' phase, I started to run and run, and run, and run.

What started as an attempt to lose some weight and change my body ended up being a totally out-of-control obsession. If for some reason I could not run, I would stress. If I got injured I would stress. If someone got in the way of my obsession, I would get grumpy and resent them.

Running became my means to having a 'normal' body. It also became the mechanism by which I could avoid being the fat kid – extremely important for me at that stage.

When you perceive something (in this instance running) as being the difference between where you were (bad) and where you are now (good), you don't want anything to stand between you and that 'thing'.

Once when I was in the middle of my obsessive running phase (I was about 15), I ran in an event at school. In the course of that race I injured some ligaments on the inside of my ankle and was subsequently instructed by a physiotherapist not to run for two weeks.

The next day I tried to run (of course) and as I did I experienced excruciating pain through my whole foot and ankle. I ran and hobbled about a hundred metres down the road and had to stop.

As I was walking dejectedly back to my house I discovered that if I walked with my injured foot in the gutter (on an angle) almost all of the pain was gone. I then discovered that I could actually jog with my foot on an angle with almost no pain.

Being the complete fruitcake I was, I figured that if I could find somewhere with enough continuous gutters, I could probably go for a decent run.

With absolutely no respect for the well-being of the ligaments in my ankle, I found a new housing estate and spent the next two weeks running with one foot in the gutter. It seemed to make sense at the time.

It is amazing what we can rationalise if we try hard enough.

Discipline is saying to yourself 'I will find an alternative while my ankle recovers (swimming maybe)' or 'I will have some time off because that is what my body needs right now'.

Obsession is saying 'I have to run no matter what, if I don't run, I will explode (mentally and physically)'.

If you experience major fear, discomfort or anxiety when your routine is interrupted, then you need to stop and re-assess.

There will always be times when (for whatever reason) you cannot exercise or you cannot train the way you would like to.

What is crucial in terms of your long-term health and fitness is not the injury itself, but how you cope emotionally with having to adapt to a less-than-ideal situation.

Remember: in control, not out of control.

IN SUMMARY

- Be disciplined, not obsessive.
- Control yourself, don't be controlled.
- If you miss a day, or seven ... it's okay!

CHAPTER 15

IT'S ABOUT YOU, NOT YOUR 'MATES'

There are unforeseen by-products of change. Sometimes your best friends will make the process harder rather than easier.

Not everybody will be happy for you as you change your body. Don't necessarily expect encouragement and support. This story will tell you that:

Once I did some work with a lady who had previously struggled to change her body. When I started working with her she had about 10 to 15 kilograms to lose along with a reasonable amount of bodyfat.

Although she is a very attractive woman, she displayed low self-esteem and lacked confidence. She had gradually stacked on the kilograms over the previous decade.

I knew that as she started to shed some of those kilograms and some of that bodyfat, she would look and feel even more attractive and hopefully, her confidence and self-esteem would improve, as is normally the case.

From the first session she showed me that she was serious about creating a new body and she followed my instructions to the letter. Her body started to look different within a week and within four weeks she had started to change quite significantly.

At about the five-week mark we had an interesting chat. She came in to train and I asked her what her friends and family thought about the fantastic progress she was making with her new body.

She looked a little sad and informed me that she got the feeling that some of her girlfriends didn't share her excitement about her fitter, leaner body. In fact, she said it was as 'if they wanted me to fail'.

"Why do you say that?" I asked.

"Well, instead of encouraging me, telling me that I look good and saying that they are happy for me, they either say nothing or they tell me that they think I am becoming obsessive because I won't eat cake with them when we go out for coffee," she said.

I encouraged her and told her not to expect that everyone (or sometimes, anyone) would share her joy with her new-found appearance and fitness level; especially when your friends are sadly out of shape themselves.

A few days later we met at a park for a training session.

"I don't know if I can do this any more," was her opening line.

"What's happened?" I asked.

"My best friend told me that since I've lost weight I am starting to look haggard.

"What does your husband say?

"Oh, he loves how I look.

"Hmmm ... is your friend overweight by any chance?

"Yes, she's about the same size as I used to be.

"Do you think perhaps she is jealous and she resents your success and maybe she is criticising you to make herself feel better?

"I never thought about it.

"Think about it because that's probably what's happening."

Incidentally, she did not look haggard; she looked fit, lean and healthy.

If you are like most people, then as soon as you start to make positive changes in your life there will be friends and acquaintances, often those you would expect to support you and make the process easier, who will (for various reasons), consciously or unconsciously, make the task of getting in shape much more difficult than it needs to be.

It is hard enough to change life-long habits without our friends hassling us all the time. As I noted earlier, if you have friends who consistently make it hard for you to achieve your goals or friends who seemingly want to sabotage your efforts to create your best body ('here try this, one little piece won't hurt you'), either confront them about it or find some friends who genuinely care about you and what you are trying to achieve.

Real friends are happy for your success. Real friends will encourage and support you.

It is my personal experience that when you are motivated and driven to achieve a goal, typically you will have more opposition than support.

Sometimes that opposition is not obvious or even verbal; it is more underlying and subtle. You know what I'm talking about.

So what is the answer to this lack of support and encouragement? The answer is for you not to be dependant on anyone when it comes to changing your body and maintaining the behaviours you know you should. It is great to have the support of a friend or mentor, but it is disastrous when you can't function without everyone in your life being supportive. You need to be single-minded, determined and independent. Your perfect body depends on you.

The truth is not everybody wants us to achieve our goals – we need to be able to deal with this fact and keep moving forward.

IN SUMMARY

- Enjoy the support of friends but don't be dependant on it.
- Not everyone will share your excitement as you create your best body.
- It's not about them, it's about you.

CHAPTER 16

SOCIAL EATING

Nothing tastes as good as being in shape feels.

As I write this chapter I am sitting on a balcony overlooking the ocean in beautiful Queensland. I am on holidays and life is good. It is a little hard to see the screen of my laptop with the sun streaming over my shoulder but I will tolerate the hardship and battle on (trooper that I am).

Two nights ago I went out for a New Year's Eve dinner with a few friends and some people I have met since I arrived here a week ago. I had not organised the dinner, didn't really know many of the guests and didn't know what the situation was in terms of ordering meals.

As it turned out it was a set menu at a Japanese restaurant and the food was abundant. While it was a pleasant evening and the company was great, I was bewildered by the sheer volume of food and even more surprised by some people's seemingly endless ability to consume that food, when they could not possibly be hungry.

By about the fifth course I started to look around the table and it dawned on me how much our lives seem to revolve around food. Food is a social experience and we are highly social beings.

In fact, many people believe that an endless supply of food and a great social outing are synonymous. The problem is that all this social eating leads to fat and unhealthy social people. Contrary to some opinions, it is possible to go to a restaurant, eat a healthy meal, avoid alcohol and not be a social misfit. If people get offended because you choose not to eat something or not to eat as much as them, let them get offended – they need to change, not you.

After a while it became evident that the way I ate bothered a few members of the group. When I wasn't hungry anymore (which was after eating the amount of food I would typically eat for dinner) I stopped eating.

While it made sense to me to stop eating if I was not hungry, it seemed to be irrational and obsessive behaviour to a few people. Obviously if I didn't eat as much as them, I could not have much of a life. Isn't it funny how people who are threatened by, or are uncomfortable because of another person's behaviour, will do their best to belittle that person in order to make themselves feel better?

You would be surprised at how many people tell me that they could not eat the way I do because they 'need to have a life'. People tell themselves and others anything in order to feel better about what they do to their body and to justify unhealthy behaviours.

As a kid I remember eating out and being told that if I didn't eat a certain thing I would offend the lady who made it, even though I had eaten an hour before. The fact that I didn't want it, like it or need it was irrelevant.

The food thing starts young. We bribe our kids with food. We shovel lollies into their mouths to keep them quiet; we create sugar junkies.

According to John Ratcliffe, who wrote an interesting book *Sugar Science*, 100 years ago the average Australian consumed approximately five pounds (2.3 kilograms) of sugar per year while the average Aussie now consumes a staggering 180 pounds (82 kilograms) of the white stuff annually.

It is no coincidence that the incidence of diabetes in this country is reaching epidemic proportions. A client of mine recently asked me if she could have barbeque sauce on her sandwich and I said it depended on the ingredients.

She brought the sauce bottle in question to her next appointment so I could read the nutritional information. To my absolute astonishment the stuff was 44 per cent sugar!

IF YOU WANT TO ACHIEVE EXCEPTIONAL THINGS YOU NEED TO BE PREPARED TO DO EXCEPTIONAL THINGS

Sometimes this means creating different rules and standards for yourself. It means being in an environment where most people are doing one thing and you are doing something different.

It may mean sitting at a table where people are eating garlic bread, lasagne and cheesecake while you have chicken and salad.

The key is to not focus on what you are missing, but rather on what you are gaining. A meal lasts a few minutes (for some people a few hours) but you have to live in that body of yours all day, every day.

People have asked me if I feel like I am missing out because I don't eat 'all the good stuff'. The truth is I feel like they are missing out because they could choose to have a fit, lean healthy physique but choose to stay fat, eat badly and do destructive things to their body.

Perspective is a funny thing.

We live in a time when you can be made to feel a social outcast if you don't do as everybody else does. In fact, I know what I am eating is the 'good stuff'; it's just that we all have different definitions of what is good.

How many times do we eat so much that before we even leave the table, we are commenting that we feel sick? Countless times I have heard people say after a massive meal 'that's it, I'm never eating again'. Why get to that point in the first place? There is no need.

A SALAD ON CHRISTMAS DAY?

Imagine a Christmas lunch where the host served up some turkey and salad and nothing else! No soup, no pudding, no sweets, no nibbles beforehand, no alcohol.

What?

That would never happen because it is socially unacceptable to do that on Christmas Day. We need to splurge on Christmas Day – it's an unwritten law.

What if we fed our body only what it needed? What if we didn't sit down to the normal feast? Would the world end? Would we all have a miserable day because we didn't overeat? Maybe we would have a better day because we didn't feel stuffed all afternoon – another freaky thought.

We are so programmed to do things a certain way that we don't even question it. We consistently perform these rituals which not only make us feel sick but turn us into an obese population.

We do it because it's the way we have always done it, and we are creatures of habit. We do it because if we don't, we're missing out.

Besides, change makes us uncomfortable.

Now before you throw this book in the bin, I am not saying that you need to avoid the family Christmas lunch or live a life of deprivation. What I am saying is that we regularly eat more than our body needs and we must have a greater level of awareness and self-control if we genuinely want to change our physiology.

It is fine to have some cake, ice-cream or a hamburger from time to time but not at every meal. Remember, almost everything that goes in will either be used for growth and repair, stored as fat or used for energy. If you eat more than you need, the only thing your body can do with it is store it as energy (fat).

It is simple maths – energy in, energy out.

If you consume 500 calories more than you need per day (on average), your body will gain approximately one pound (.45kg) of fat per week.

So, if we eat more than we need, guess where it is going? That's right – straight on those little love handles. So how do you reduce the excess intake? Here's a start:

Learn to differentiate between cravings and genuine hunger.

Why do we get hungry 30 minutes after we eat a big meal? We don't. That hunger you think you feel is nothing more than a craving related to your blood sugar level. Genuine hunger is a sign that your body is at a point where it needs energy – food.

If you ate a meal 30 minutes ago and you feel like eating again I can assure you that what you are experiencing is not hunger. Notice how when you are 'peckish' 30 minutes after dinner that you often want something sweet – we never crave for tuna or broccoli after our evening meal, do we?

We are so used to eating at the slightest hint of a craving that we have lost the ability to even recognise genuine hunger.

Many people never experience real hunger because they never stop eating. These are often the same people who take diet pills, appetite suppressants and, eventually, the surgical option.

IN SUMMARY

- Being social doesn't mean being a glutton.
- You can say 'no', without offending.
- Don't eat what you don't need.
- Your instincts are rarely wrong. Listen to your body.
- Don't worry about what people think, worry about your health.

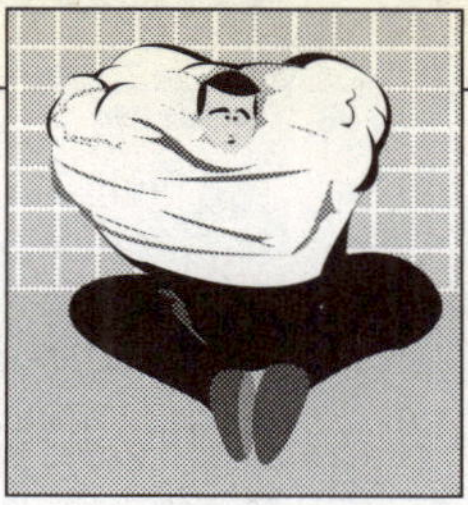

CHAPTER 17

DON'T CONFUSE THE SIX-PACK WITH INNER PEACE

Fixing the body won't necessarily fix everything else.

Over the years I have seen many people achieve amazing things with their lifestyle, relationships, emotions, attitudes and, of course, their body. But it doesn't always work all ways.

I have seen people who were at absolute breaking point (physically, emotionally and psychologically) re-invent themselves in a matter of months. I am still constantly amazed at how much people can change and what they can achieve in a relatively short period of time when they are totally focused.

The human body is a truly amazing, adaptable thing. I consider myself to have one of the most rewarding jobs in the world and I love being able to play a small role in helping people turn their life around. However, one thing happens quite regularly that really bothers me.

With some people there seems to be an inversely proportional relationship – the better they look, the more miserable, stressed and unhappy they become.

Every week I talk to people who are desperate to lose weight and change their body. After spending 10 or 15 minutes with some of them I realise that, while they do need to lose weight and get in shape, the state of their body is probably the least of their problems. Everyone has 'issues' but some people have much bigger problems than what size jeans they are wearing at the moment.

This does not mean that you need to wait until you have no issues before you create your best body. It means that you must understand that being in better physical condition will not necessarily solve all of your problems.

As obvious as this may seem, you would be astounded at how many people become more and more depressed as they lose weight because, even though their pants are getting looser, they still seem to have all of the issues and problems that they thought would disappear with their love handles.

Yes, being in better physical condition can impact positively in many areas of your life but it is not a quick fix for every issue or problem.

Many people believe that if they can change their body, then their dysfunctional relationship with their partner will be miraculously transformed. Unfortunately they often lose the weight only to find things are exactly the same or worse because they have not addressed the real issues.

IN SUMMARY

- We can't fix emotional and psychological problems with a physical solution.

CHAPTER 18

DON'T BE A SPOILSPORT

There's no point in toiling if you don't enjoy the outcome. Enjoy your success.

Imagine you are a player in a basketball team and for the last 10 months you and your team-mates have been training night and day with the single-minded focus of achieving the ultimate goal; a premiership victory.

Finally the big day arrives. After nearly a year of gruelling tryouts, pre-season training, overcoming injuries, unbelievable pressure, sacrifice and heartache, you make it all the way through the home and away series, through the finals series and now, it is finally down to two teams.

You have made it to the Grand Final.

The night before the big game you can hardly sleep, you are so excited. You toss and turn all night picturing yourself holding that premiership cup, having achieved your sporting dream. You go through every possible scenario in your mind and deal with every possible obstacle standing between you and that goal.

You are ready.

Finally the moment arrives; the game is on. You play like a champion, the team is amazing, everyone plays above form, the final buzzer goes and victory is yours.

Just as you are about to start enjoying the spoils of your success and celebrate achieving your ultimate (sporting) goal, the coach quickly hustles the whole team off court and into the change room before anybody has a chance to do anything.

You are just about to lead the team in a rousing rendition of the club song when the coach starts screaming at the whole team for some mistakes made early in the game and within minutes he is ranting and raving like an irrational idiot.

He proceeds to inform you that even though you won the game, you under-achieved and there will be an early morning training session the next day. He tells you that you haven't fulfilled your potential, you wasted opportunities and you have no real reason to celebrate. All of a sudden the mood goes from one of euphoria to one of absolute disappointment and disillusion.

Can you imagine this happening in real life? Of course it wouldn't.

As a team you worked hard, you sacrificed, took chances, got uncomfortable, overcame adversity and you achieved your goal. So why would the coach be anything but deliriously happy?

Once you have achieved a goal, once you have got where you wanted to go, you need to be able to sit back and acknowledge the achievement and be happy and satisfied that you have accomplished what you set out to.

Guess what? The scenario I have described happens every single day; sometimes you are that crazy coach. You achieve a certain level of success but you don't let yourself enjoy what you have achieved.

We don't acknowledge how well we have done and we don't let ourselves experience that sense of satisfaction and accomplishment that should come when we reach our goals. Instead we keep moving the goals and changing the rules.

Take the story of 'Pauline', a woman I have trained for nine years.

> Monday to Saturday, for an hour every day she lifts, jumps, runs, skips and stretches her way through workout after workout with me.
>
> She's in her 50s, but has a body that most 25-year-olds would be very happy with. In nine years she has transformed herself from a fat, overweight, unfit, unmotivated cake-eating machine into an exceptionally fit, strong and lean athlete.
>
> She has lost 20-plus kilograms, reduced her bodyfat from more than 40 per cent to 20 per cent, increased her running distance from 10 metres to a half-marathon (21 kilometres) and has gained so much strength that she is now stronger than many men I have trained (also significantly more determined).
>
> Like me, she also has a naturally endomorphic body type, meaning that she has a natural genetic disposition to gain bodyfat easily.
>
> So you would probably assume that this endomorph who has achieved a body beyond her wildest dreams at an age when many people are reclining into their retirement years would be overwhelmingly happy with her 'new body.'
>
> Wrong.
>
> Never lean enough, never light enough, runs too slow, fat stomach, tuckshop arms, fat legs – if you heard her describe herself without actually seeing her, you would think she was morbidly obese, hideously ugly and at death's door.
>
> Sound familiar?
>
> As long as I have known her, she has been making it impossible to be happy.
>
> Some time ago we went for a run. Before the session, the

furthest she had ever run in her life was about 12 kilometres.

On this particular day we ran 15 kilometres and she did it easily – she could have run 20 kilometres.

We got back and I was ecstatic for her – 53 years old, didn't start exercising until she was well into her 40s; here she was doing something most 20-year-olds couldn't do and something she had never achieved in her life.

I was so excited I started telling her how amazing she was, what a great job she had done and how happy she should be with herself.

Instead of being thrilled with her achievement her first comment was that she "runs like an old woman and is too slow." Like the basketball coach, she had turned victory into defeat.

When you experience success let yourself enjoy it. If you don't learn to enjoy the triumphs you will be perpetually miserable and forever trying to achieve the unachievable.

IN SUMMARY

- When you succeed, enjoy it.
- Congratulate yourself.
- Winning is so much fun.
- Stop moving the goalposts.
- Stop making it impossible for yourself to be happy.

SECTION FOUR

CASE STUDIES

Every day I work with people who teach me, motivate me, inspire me, frustrate me, shock me and occasionally make me laugh. Here are a few stories.

Chapter 19	**Jan & Ian: older bodies younger attitude**	146
Chapter 20	**'Maggie': a turn for the better**	151
Chapter 21	**Craig: the sick obsessive**	154
Chapter 22	**'Bill': finding the right program for you**	157
Chapter 23	**Jim Solopitias**	159
Chapter 24	**Artie Kalnins**	161
Chapter 25	**Captain Inconsistency**	163
Chapter 26	**'George': too much training, too little recovery**	165

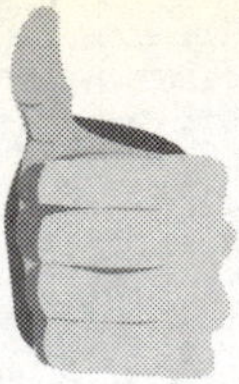

CHAPTER 19

JAN & IAN: OLDER BODIES, YOUNGER ATTITUDE

This amazing sixty-something couple are a perfect example of how a great attitude can keep you much younger than your years.

Some years ago I started training a woman who was 54 years old. While she was not particularly out of shape for someone in her 50s, she was not particularly fit or strong either.

Within a short time she began to make amazing progress, getting fitter and stronger by the week. What surprised me most about Jan was that, unlike many people I had worked with, she didn't have an 'old' mentality.

She didn't seem to think like a lot of people do once they hit 50 and beyond. She didn't provide me with the often heard 'remember I'm an old woman' line, instead she approached every session and challenge with the enthusiasm of an excitable kid.

It was so refreshing to train someone who didn't come into the process thinking and behaving old, or limiting herself before she had even started. Some people hit a certain age and instantly adopt an 'old' mentality; not long after this it is usually reflected in their physiology. If you think and behave like an 'old' person, pretty soon you'll be one!

Jan was the opposite. She was prepared to exercise, whatever that was going to be. She lifted weights, boxed, ran, stretched, rode bikes and did whatever was asked of her.

She didn't rationalise whether or not each workout was appropriate for someone her age, she just did what I set for her. Within a short amount of time she began to make amazing changes to her body and her life.

At a time when many people are quietly 'sliding into their retirement years' this average woman with an amazing attitude decided she would get fitter, stronger and leaner than she ever had before. Not fit for an older person, fit for a person of any age.

A year or so after I began working with Jan we were talking in the gym one day and she mentioned to me that she thought my job was something that would be fun and rewarding to do.

It was just a passing comment but it was from the heart so I suggested that she could do some formal study, get qualified and become a trainer. I explained to her the study and qualification process and told her that when she qualified I would give her a job!

Admittedly she was a little hesitant, as not too many people undertake study in their mid-50s and take up a new career as they head into their 60s.

I later discovered she was not really worried about whether or not she could do it; she was more concerned at how people might react to being trained by an 'old' trainer.

Jan is now 63 years old and has been working with me, helping people change their bodies and their lives, for the past five years. She is a fantastic trainer, mentor and teacher. I don't mean fantastic for her age, I mean fantastic – full stop.

This grandmother, who runs 10 kilometres at a time, does push ups with the boys and rides her bike up to 200 kilometres in one hit, is an absolute inspiration to everyone she comes into contact with.

She is an inspiration, not because she is extraordinarily gifted, but because she has an amazing attitude and an amazing outlook on life. I recently told her I want her to work with me until she is at least 80. “Okay,” she said.

Once a week a group of my trainers get together to do a killer fitness session. The session is an hour of pain and is not for the faint-hearted.

These sessions are usually competitive and designed to take the participants to the ‘edge’ for a bit of a look. Every week without fail Jan is the first one ready to train. Aside from her, the average age of the group is around 30.

While most people her age would not even consider getting involved in something so ‘inappropriate’ for a 63-year-old, she is sweating her backside off and not trying to rationalise whether or not her behaviour is ‘sensible’ or ‘normal’.

What society generally tells our older generation is that if they want to exercise it’s really just a matter of deciding which bowling club is the most convenient (apologies to the bowling fraternity).

I believe the biggest thing holding back our older generation is not their potential to drastically change their bodies or to improve their fitness levels but the condescending and patronising attitudes held by many so-called experts who seem determined to put anyone over 50 in a little protective cocoon so they will not harm themselves.

It is much more harmful to do nothing than to do something. If you are 60 and you have never gone surfing, take it up!

So many health professionals do not really understand the huge potential for change and adaptation human beings possess at any age. Yes, we need to exercise caution and common sense but no, we don’t need to put the slippers on and wait for the grim reaper.

If (some of) our medical profession were to prescribe dumbbells and exercise balls instead of drugs we would (in my opinion) have a much healthier, happier and more functional older population.

Before you doctors start jumping up and down, I acknowledge that there is a place and a time for a pharmaceutical approach but I also believe that in many instances medication is prescribed when an exercise-based approach may be a viable and even more effective option.

Over the past 10 years there have been countless studies conducted which have repeatedly demonstrated the ability that people have to change their level of strength and fitness even into their 90s.

I have personally worked with people aged in their 80s who have more than doubled their strength in two or three months.

Did you know that a 90-year-old can build muscle? They can.

About four years ago Jan's husband Ian decided that after mucking around with a few weights at home for a while he would come into the gym and do a few supervised training sessions in order to learn how to train more effectively and productively. When he first started training (following a structured program) he was 60.

Not unlike his amazing wife, he too possessed a refreshing outlook and also began to make unbelievable progress. So astounding was his development that I decided to do some testing on him for a research project I was completing for my university studies on muscle wasting in the elderly.

What my research revealed was that this 62-year-old (he's now 66) was the fittest, strongest and leanest he had ever been in his life and that physiologically he had a body leaner, stronger and fitter than most 20-year-olds.

Looking at photos of him from when he was in his 20s it is evident that he has significantly more muscle now than he had 40 years ago, when he was supposedly in his prime. That's not meant to happen. Freaky stuff.

During the testing he was required to perform maximum chin-ups (pulling your bodyweight up to a bar) and maximum push-ups. In the chin-ups he scored 25 full repetitions (the average score for someone in their 20s is about five to 10 repetitions) and in the push-ups he scored 50 (the average score for someone in their 20s is around 20 to 30 repetitions).

For those of you who are wondering about the technique used for the chin-ups and push-ups, they were full movements, not a modified version for older people.

Jan and Ian's story is not typical, but it could be. We often see a rapid physical decline with some of our population, often around 55 to 65 years old. This is simply because they go from being relatively active to being a lounge lizard within a short period of time.

It is not about their age, it is about their activity level. Take, for example, a guy who has been working for the last 45 years. He started working as an apprentice carpenter when he was 15 and now is 60 and hanging up the tool belt.

Last week he was relatively active for 10 hours a day, this week his biggest issues are which TV station he will watch and how he can place his bets without actually getting off the couch. Despite the fact that he has gone from high to low activity levels, he continues to consume the same amount of food as always, through habit, or boredom.

Six months down the track he needs to have the couch surgically removed from his backside, has put on 10 kilograms of fat, has lost a significant amount of muscle, his fitness level has plummeted and he is starting to fall into depression because he hates the way he looks and feels.

The reason many people seem to age drastically at certain stages of life usually has more to do with lifestyle and behavioural change than it has to do with some pre-determined, age-related biological factor (as many people believe).

People who have a healthy lifestyle, remain active and eat intelligently and appropriately for their needs don't generally experience the same rapid deterioration that so many others do.

CHAPTER 20

'MAGGIE': A TURN FOR THE BETTER

It's not about how much we train; it's about whether or not we stimulate our body the right way.

About seven years ago I had an appointment with a woman who was already exercising at another gym but was frustrated with her lack of progress. Let's call her 'Maggie'.

As usual we spent an hour or so discussing what she was currently doing in terms of exercise and diet and what she wanted to change about her body.

In the course of the conversation I discovered that she was already doing 14 hours of exercise per week, every week. For the previous two years she had been doing morning and evening aerobics classes, the same classes, same instructors, essentially the same workout, day in, day out.

Apart from the odd missed class, she had been doing the same 14 hours per week of aerobics for two years. No running, no bike, no boxing, no incline walks, no weight training, no variety.

I discovered that she ate on average two (no, it's not a misprint) meals per day, all of this at a bodyweight of just under 90 kilograms! I also learned that while she had initially lost some weight, her body had remained the same for about 18 months.

On informing her that she needed to change her program completely in order to stimulate her body to change, she looked a little nervous. My explanation to her was that she needed to eat more and exercise less (but differently). That went down well.

The program I wanted her to follow consisted of five one-hour training sessions per week, instead of the normal 14 hours of aerobics, and five small meals per day instead of the usual two.

I explained why her body wasn't changing from an exercise and also a dietary perspective. I felt that she had all but destroyed her metabolism by under-eating for so long. She needed to re-ignite her metabolism and to provide her body with a reason to change (different training and eating).

Despite the fact that this woman is highly intelligent (she is a qualified physiotherapist and occupational therapist) and it all seemed to make sense to her, she informed me that she didn't think she could 'do it'. She told me that she loved her aerobics classes and she didn't want to give them up.

I realised at this point how emotional we can be about exercise. Here is a woman who is doing the same thing over and over and getting no results, yet she didn't want to change her program because she had an emotional attachment to aerobics.

Sometimes we need a balance between doing the things we love to do with our exercise, in this case aerobics, and the things which will produce the results we want.

It amazed me that even though she hated her body and she was not getting the results she desired, she was very hesitant to change her exercise routine – even after nearly two years of no results!

My question to her was why did she come to me if she didn't want me to change her program? The answer was that she hoped

I might give her something additional to her existing training schedule which might do the trick. Just what she needed; two meals per day, 14 aerobics classes per week and some personal training sessions!

After some intense negotiating I persuaded her to follow my suggested plan for four weeks. I told her that if she followed it to the letter and it didn't work I would refund all of her money.

For four weeks she ate five small meals and did five, one-hour training sessions per week. None of the sessions over the four-week period were the same.

Although she found it very difficult to exercise less and have two days per week off training, she stayed with the program. Interestingly, she told me that she found the five hours of training with me more taxing than the 14 hours of aerobics she was previously doing.

In the four weeks she lost six kilograms, her overall energy level went through the roof, her fitness improved considerably and she was very happy with her achievement.

It had taken her four weeks to realise that what she was emotionally and psychologically comfortable with was not going to produce the physical results she desired.

The happy ending is that after six months she had lost about 20 kilograms doing what works rather than what she was comfortable with.

She stopped working as a physiotherapist and now works for me as a trainer – making people do what I made her do. Life's funny like that.

CHAPTER 21

CRAIG: THE SICK OBSESSIVE

Sometimes doing less will give us more. I learned this the hard way.

When I set up my first centre in 1991 I was lifting weights six days per week (and had been for years) and was quite heavily into bodybuilding.

At the time I was working 60 to 70 hours per week training people, lecturing and generally trying to run and grow a new business. At that stage of my business development, I was head trainer, administration manager, marketing manager, mirror cleaner, toilet cleaner and maintenance man.

About two weeks after I opened the doors of my business I got the flu and was quite sick. As I had no staff, I figured I had no option but to train people (from a distance) considering I had to pay the bills and ensure my clients didn't miss their workouts. The doctor told me that I should not exercise at all and I should probably have a week off work also.

What would he know?

Being the mental giant that I am, I decided that I would do a workout half an hour after I got back from the doctor. I remember doing a warm-up set of shoulder press, putting the weights down and then almost passing out. I had to lie down for about 30 minutes before I could stand up.

When I finally got back on my feet I made an amazing decision (for me); I would let myself get better (freaky), give myself a week off training and concentrate my limited energy solely on my new business for a week.

Exactly seven days after that decision I did my first workout back in the gym and another amazing thing happened – I lifted heavier weights than I had in a year and I had so much energy it was unbelievable. Being as sharp as a bowling ball, I reasoned that I must have just been having a really good day and didn't think too much of it.

As I was regularly getting to work at 5am and leaving at 9pm and was constantly tired, I resigned myself to the fact that my own training would have to take a backseat to the business for a while.

Reluctantly I decided that I would only train three days per week for three months and do my best to maintain my size and strength over that time.

While it messed with my head to halve my workout schedule, I figured that once my business was more self-sufficient I would have enough time to train 'normally' (six days) and regain what muscle and strength I had lost. Good plan.

The first week my training partner thought I had started taking steroids. I was strong, really strong. In the first eight weeks of my 'maintenance' program I gained three kilos while my bodyfat stayed the same.

Every week I seemed to get stronger in all lifts and every time I got to work out I felt fresh and full of energy for the first time in a long time.

It didn't take me too long to figure out that my body enjoyed four recovery days a week more than it did one. It also didn't take me long to deduce that I had been perpetually fatigued and overtrained for a long time.

I realised that what my head wanted and what my body needed were two different things.

Don't assume that if three workouts are good, then six will be twice as good. It is not always the case, particularly when we are talking about more intense exercise.

CHAPTER 22

'BILL': FINDING THE BEST PROGRAM FOR YOU

Make sure you follow a program which is specific to your needs (goals, age, fitness level, level of health) otherwise you might find the process to be an exercise in frustration.

Recently one of my friends rang me and asked if I would talk to his father 'Bill', about his exercise program. The father was obese and hypertensive (high blood pressure) and had been told by his doctor about six months earlier that he needed to lose 30 kilograms urgently or he could go to God any time.

The son informed me that following the meeting with the doctor his dad had joined a gym and had been following his gym program religiously but was disappointed with the lack of results. He had lost two kilograms in six months. I would be disappointed too.

When I met with Bill, the first thing I did was look at the program he had been following. It took about 30 seconds to figure out why he wasn't achieving his goals. A 58-year-old guy who needs to lose weight and increase his fitness level urgently should be following an exercise program composed largely of low-impact, low-intensity cardio vascular exercise. In other words, get your heart rate up a little, get sweaty and do it regularly.

Instead of his ideal program he was prescribed a workout that was basically a bodybuilding program – weights three days per week, with a five-minute bike warm-up at the start of each workout.

This is a great program if you are a 20-year-old footballer who wants to bulk up over summer but not if you are a 58-year-old, hypertensive, unfit, obese guy who needs to drop 30 kilograms.

Not surprisingly, his program was written by a bodybuilder – no offence to the bodybuilding fraternity, there are many bodybuilders who are good trainers. Even though this guy had a good attitude, trained consistently and made the effort, he was never going to achieve optimal results because he was following a program which was not appropriate for him.

As I write this he has been following his new program for six weeks and has lost a further 6.5 kilograms. He is not training any harder or for any longer, it's just that he is stimulating his body the right way and following an appropriate program.

He is doing the right thing for him.

Make sure that you do the right thing for you.

Do not assume your neighbour's program is right for you.

CHAPTER 23

JIM SOLOPITIAS

Take your mind there and your body will follow. Jim did… and re-invented himself in five months.

When I first met Jim Solopitias in January 2004, he was out of shape, out of motivation and seemingly out of answers. He had progressively gained more and more weight over the years and the day I met him he was an unhappy 36-year-old, weighing 114 kilograms with a bodyfat level approaching 40 per cent.

Like many people, Jim seemed to hate his body and was not enjoying life. Not only did the weight affect him physically but it had affected virtually every area of his life; work, relationships, social life and his overall level of confidence, motivation and self-esteem.

Pretty normal stuff when you're embarrassed by your body.

After chatting to him for 30 minutes I knew that he would get results and probably get them fast. Sometimes when I meet people I can sense that they have arrived at that place we all need to get to (psychologically) before we are going to create real change.

He was there.

Jim started his new approach to life on February 3, 2004. Five small healthy meals a day, six exercise sessions per week (two with a trainer), a new attitude, a new plan, a new structure, a new level of understanding and some genuine excitement and hope. I find that when people get genuinely excited, and that excitement has a sensible plan attached to it, they will invariably get results.

Now five months later the guy with the body he hated is 28 kilograms lighter, has 19 per cent bodyfat and is bursting with energy, excitement and enthusiasm about what the future holds.

I saw him in the gym recently and he looks like a completely different person. He informed me that many friends have walked right past because they don't recognise him. He also told me that he is now studying to work in the fitness industry!

Why did he create great results in such a short time?

He made no excuses, he was ready to do what was necessary and he was consistent in his approach.

"Now that I know what I can achieve, I wonder what I was doing for so long."

– Jim Solopitias

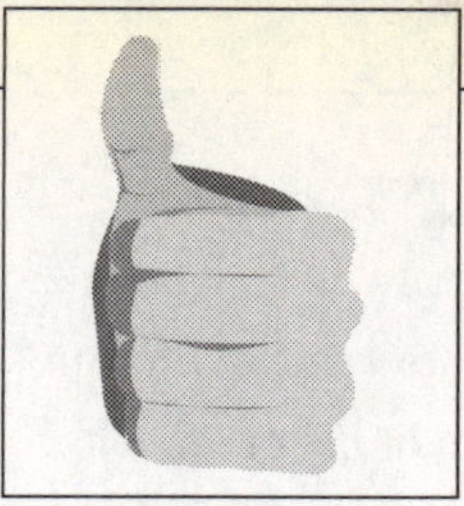

CHAPTER 24

ARTIE KALNINS

One night he was in one of my seminars, the next day he was in my gym. Six months later and twenty kilos lighter, the 46 year-old fat bloke is now a finely tuned athlete.

Late in 2003 I gave a presentation to a few hundred people. I spoke about the usual stuff; food, exercise, attitude, genetics, psychology – a standard presentation.

Driving home from the talk I critiqued myself – 'not too bad, not amazing, could change this, could do that better … hopefully someone got something out of it'.

The next morning a guy rang me.

"G'day, I was at your talk last night and I'm pumped. I'm ready to re-invent myself, any chance we can meet today?" It was Artie Kalnins.

At 193 centimetres and 121 kilograms, Artie cast an imposing shadow in the doorway of my office. He was carrying too much fat, too much weight, was unhealthy, hated how he looked, was consistently low on energy and generally wasn't a happy camper.

We spent only 30 minutes together and he informed me that my seminar had "been a kick in the arse" and that he was ready to do whatever was necessary to achieve life-long change.

I discovered that both of his parents have a history of heart disease. At the age of 46, Artie did not want to end up like his father who had undergone a triple bypass.

Good thinking.

He also informed me that his partner Charlene wasn't as partial to the 46-year-old big fat bloke as she was to the lean mean machine she had hooked up with years earlier.

The interesting thing about Artie was that he had previously worked in gyms helping people get in shape! When you look into it, you would be amazed to discover how many health and fitness professionals wake up one day living in a body they hate.

For Artie the actual physiological changes happened quite quickly once he got to that point emotionally and psychologically where he was really ready to commit; he shed 20 kilograms and a truckload of body fat within six months. These days he moves more like a panther (okay, a really big panther) than a middle-aged fat bloke, is bursting with energy, looks great and has a new lease on life.

Although my seminar was the catalyst for change for Artie, it is important to keep in mind that while there were hundreds of people in attendance, he was the only who contacted me and I wouldn't mind betting he was the only one who actually did something significant with the information. It's not about knowing, it's about doing.

"As soon as I got my thinking right,
the rest was easy."

– Artie Kalnins

CHAPTER 25

CAPTAIN INCONSISTENCY

Sometimes we need stop thinking about it and talking about it and actually do something. And when we start, we need to keep doing whatever it was we started.

I have a close friend who has been telling me for the last 10 years that he needs to lose weight. Every year (at least once or twice a year) we have the same discussion about the same issues (his body, lifestyle, diet, exercise habits). Every time we chat I tell him what I think he should be doing and why. I also tell him that he is welcome to train at one of my gyms and again, I answer the same questions he has asked me many times before.

Every year he repeats the cycle: starts a program, stops a program, eats badly, eats well, loses a few kilos, gains a few more, makes excuses, gets depressed, comes back to me and asks the same questions I've answered many times.

Last year I told him I didn't want to talk to him about his body any more. He asked me whether or not I had given up on him. I told him that there comes a point when we need to stop talking and start doing and I felt that he was at that point. At first he was upset with me and did not want to acknowledge that what I had said might be true, later that day he rang me to thank me for telling him what he needed to hear. He told me that when he put his ego on hold and thought through what I had said, a switch came on and he realised how much time he had wasted.

Progress at last.

He's now been training well and eating well for nearly a year and he has never looked or felt better.

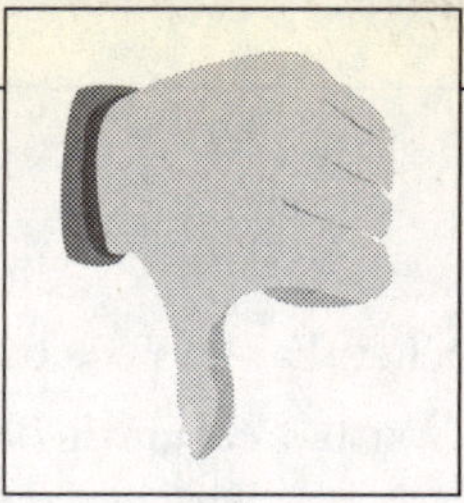

CHAPTER 26

'GEORGE': TOO MUCH TRAINING, TOO LITTLE RECOVERY

What our body needs and what we are 'comfortable' with are often two different things. Sometimes people do too little, George did too much.

Recently I had a bodybuilder come to see me about his training because he wanted some advice regarding his lack of progress with his chest development (bodybuilders get judged in competition on each individual body part as well as overall appearance). 'George' felt that this chest wasn't progressing compared with the rest of his body. When he outlined his program to me, I told him the solution was simple – train his chest less because it was overtrained. He freaked out.

I explained that his body was probably in a constant state of disrepair because he was perpetually overtrained. When you are trying to stimulate a muscle group to gain size and strength, recovery time and nutrition are at least as important, in terms of getting results, as the actual training.

On hearing this he told me that he understood what I was saying (intellectually) but he wasn't comfortable with it (emotionally). As I said, you don't need to be comfortable with it.

He had an irrational belief that 'more is better' and by doing 'less' he would go backwards. With even a little basic scientific knowledge he would understand that, when it comes to growing muscle, recovery and nutrition are just as important as the actual training.

Lifting weights doesn't make you bigger. Lifting weights the right way, with the right diet and appropriate recovery makes you bigger (if you have the right genetics).

Sometimes we are so intent on changing our body and getting results quickly that we get ourselves into an overtrained state quite easily. Don't assume that six workouts per week are twice as good as three.

If you are frequently tired or sore before you even start your workout or, if you rarely feel fresh or 'brand new', then there is a chance that you are overtrained.

When we are overtrained the quality of our training decreases, we are more susceptible to injury and the results come to a grinding halt. Then what often happens is that as the results fall away, people often panic, tend to train even harder and get into a state where they are totally overtrained and usually end up injured.

In my experience those most likely to overtrain are people who have made a decision to get in shape in the last few months and are following the 'more is better' principle.

SECTION FIVE

A PERSONAL ACCOUNT

You might think all that's gone before is theory. To prove the theory, I asked a person who was desperate to change, to put herself through the wringer. Marlo came, she did the work, and on the following pages is her very revealing diary, in her own words. Her story is very common. She showed enormous courage and persistence to work through the issues she needed to address. Now her challenge is to keep to it, to make it normal.

CHAPTER 27

MARLO

At the beginning of the development phase of this book, Marlo, 28, an account manager in a publishing company, volunteered to try the Craig Harper system, full on, for 28 days. This is her story.

Monday, 5th July 2004

It's 12.19 Tuesday morning, I got home from work half an hour ago. It was a bloody long day, one that I would choose to forget normally. But after receiving the news late last week – Friday I think that I was going to open my world up to others like I have never before, I thought it might be an idea to capture my thought process along the way. I need to get back into the habit of writing. It has been too long since I penned anything; especially about me and what it is I'm feeling, how I see the world – even if it is not while travelling, what affects me, when and how and everything in between.

The next month may (and should) change my life forever.

Wow. It's quietly exciting. Imagine that. I've always thought that this day would come. How fortunate. Timing. Fate is everything sometimes.

So what do I expect shall happen?

Good question – I suspect I'm going to touch deep down – to the root of all 'eating evil'. To the real problems – self-esteem, confidence, depression, stress, relationships, work, home, family, LIFE!

How can you not change the way you are by not looking at all these areas of your life? You just can't. So it's time. Time to embrace the change, the challenges and the unknown.

The unknown of my inner strength and weakness, my ability to push through – the 'will power', the determination, the courage to confront. It will all be tested at one point, I do not doubt it. Yes it's scary, frightening in fact. I hope I can achieve. Setting my expectations at a reasonable level as to reach, struggle at times, but to get there in the end. Sometimes I disappoint myself with unrealistic expectations. Part of the problem I reckon.

What are my goals? What am I going to achieve? How? Who will play a part? Will I have the inner strength? I'm not so worried about physical challenges as I think I have the strength to tough it out, but mentally – will I make it? Will I achieve? Will I be successful? Will it work out for me? How long will it take?

'How good it must feel to be so young and free.'
– Ben Harper

I hope over the next month I can answer all these questions, dispel all my fears, gain strength – both inner and physical – and most importantly achieve what it is that I've been longing for an eternity – happiness with my body, my life and myself ...

There is a long way to go – time will tell. Mind you. There are so many things I want to achieve that for some are so simple, but others like climbing the Himalayas. Here are a few things I want to achieve.

- Buy a pair of jeans (and women's at that).
- Wear a swimsuit & feel good about it.
- Go to the beach and have fun.
- Run 10kms without feeling like my heart is going to explode.

- Feel confident walking into a room full of strangers.
- Buy any sort of pants, trousers.
- Shopping in general.
- Feel sexy naked without the lights off.
- Enjoy looking at myself (in the mirror) without condemnation.
- Feel confident to stand up for myself – at work and at home.
- Feeling good.
- Smiling infectiously.
- Having clear and radiant skin.
- General health, losing fat, losing weight.
- Detoxing.

I'm sure the list will grow. Some things will become less important than others, some will be more important. Time will tell.

Tuesday, 6th July 2004

Too exhausted to write. Staying at a friend's place. Catching up, wondering at the ways of the world, love, life, travels and what it means at the end of the day. The question that we often ask ourselves. Is it an 'age' thing? Are we at 'that' age and what exactly does that mean. This is something I need to explore. Sleep time.

Friday, 16th July 2004

It's a vicious cycle of hope, loneliness, idealism and romanticism.

Monday, 2nd August 2004

What a day, back at work, head spinning – but calm. Holidays 'have come and gone' and now my focus is on the next 28 days.

It's going to be tough. The biggest challenge will be to maintain enthusiasm, motivation and the calm I feel now. It has been two days – no alcohol. Now that's pretty good – and I feel better for it. Might be tough come the weekend. It's quite isolating really, how much my life revolves around going out, pubs, parties, dinner, food – drinking! I will have to find other things to do.

Problem I see with that is – loneliness, not too many people I know live healthy lifestyles, actually, not that that means it's right or wrong – just different.

First training session – Craig, what a great bloke, approachable, easy going, understanding, no bullshit – I like him, he knows his stuff, he enjoys what he does and he is making a difference to many people's lives. Sounds like what I'm striving for.

The gym – DAUNTING! As always – gyms make me nervous, mirrors, mirrors, mirrors.

I just don't get it. I'm there because I don't like the way I look. I DON'T WANT TO LOOK AT MYSELF. Surely that's not a hard concept to grasp. I'm sure I'll get use to it, always hard at the start. Something new, something different, confronting – seeing all the fit, toned bodies is daunting – but then again, there were not-so-fit bodies as well – relief, it's not all that bad.

I was nervous, unfit, hurting and puffing, felt like my heart was going to explode, I wanted to vomit.

IS THIS GOOD FOR YOU?

Of course it is! That's why it hurts so much.

IT IS GOING TO BE A LONG 28 DAYS.

Training – support (and having it) really does help. It is going to be fun.

Biggest challenge – FOOD.

Maintaining motivation – not an issue yet, but obviously has been in the past.

Have a goal – losing 16 kilos (eventually).

Tuesday, 3rd August 2004

Remnants of full moon, feeling a little sad, always do – strange how that happens at this time of the month.

Focus. Focus. Focus.

Went for a run today. Struggled. Legs felt so heavy; heart felt like it was going to explode. Body aching. Coping with the food today. It's at 3pm as always that my mind wonders and a chocolate seems like a good option. Not today though. Which is good news. Plus a second workout session.

Wednesday, 4th August 2004

YOU HAVE TO DO IT EVEN WHEN YOU DON'T WANT TO!

It is 12.17am Thursday – just been for a run. 32 mins and it hurt. But I am so glad I made myself do it.

Long day – work, meetings, emails, clients, meeting up with friends, talk, talk, talk. Half-hour to clear my head. Did wonders – why is it so hard to get out and run when it really does make you feel better?

The answer is simple and in the form of my housemate when I was heading out at 11.22pm "What the hell? Where are you going?"

"For a run," I answer.

" Are you nuts?" she asks, followed by "crazy woman".

Yep, maybe crazy but one who wants to lose 16kgs and unfortunately – it is not going to lose itself.

Wednesday, 18th August 2004

I haven't written in a while – even though many thoughts run through my mind. I'm now over two weeks into my 28-day 'change of life' challenge. AND IT'S TOUGH.

Tough to maintain momentum.

Tough to be excited.

Tough to get out of bed when its 2°C and there are two inches of ice on my car window, but hardest of all – TOUGH to realise that to achieve what I want and then maintain it, that this is going to HAVE to be forever. Not just 28 days. Wow. That is depressing. I'm going to have to eat like this, exercise like mad, push myself to do things I don't want to do, not just for 28 days but FOREVER.

Will it get easier? Will it one day be fun? Will I not long for a piece of chocolate mud cake, a beer and a piece of pizza? Will I one day have the realisation that all those things are, in fact, not good for me and that I do not need them. I know I don't need them BUT I WANT THEM!

Why, oh why, can't I be the person I want to be without having to put myself through this?

I go to the gym and I look at myself and I hate what I see. In fact I cannot look at myself. It makes me want to cry – seriously. I look around at the fit, good-looking energetic bodies and I think I wish that was me now – and I often wonder what do they do to maintain their perfect body (well, to me they have perfect bodies, maybe they are just as insecure as I am).

Are we all looking around at each other longing to be something else? Maybe that is just me?

This is the realisation – I have a long way to go.

Someone said to me today "you only have two weeks to go" and I replied "No I don't, I have the rest of my life".

This is it – "the rest of my life".

Boy, that is hard – harder than I ever thought.

Running a 2km time trial last night I was thinking many things:

- Counting my steps (just to get through it).
- Why am I so fat and unfit?
- What did I do to deserve to be so fat and unfit?
- I want to vomit.
- I can't breathe.
- I want to cry (in fact, maybe I had to hold myself back from crying).

I got through it – don't know how I did it really. Some inner strength I never knew I had maybe. I hope I continue to find that inner strength. I need it. Maybe I have it. Hiding somewhere deep down. I suspect it is in the vision I have of myself. I suspect it's when I get repulsed with a photo of myself or looking in a mirror at myself.

Where do these 'dark' thoughts come from?

How can I get rid of them?

Why do I hate myself so much?

Is anyone going to love me, for just being me – if I don't love myself?

It is sad to write this, isn't it?

Well, it's sad for me to think some days too.

Food is one problem among many. But who would have thought a piece of chocolate mud cake would beat me. I knew when I ate it that it was bad for me. So why did I eat it?

I AM WEAK. It just looked so good. I wish I could vomit. "Food, food, food, glorious food".

Why do they make food that isn't good for you?

WHY? WHY? WHY?

So many questions – I'm searching for the answers, they are not coming yet but I hope they do soon.

Thursday, 19th August 2004

Worked out hard today. Ate well. Felt great.

Still no alcohol and that for me is an achievement in itself. If I can make it through this weekend I reckon I'll be doing okay. In fact, I know I'll be doing okay.

What a comfort.

Sweated, pumped, hurt, run, punched, treaded, lifted, pumped and pumped some more.

It is a long road – am I going to ever get there? I'm scared, what is riding on it?

I am searching for something, what happens if I don't find it? Will happiness find me? Wouldn't that be great – one day?

It's good to know that asking the question may get me a step closer. Some people go through life never asking IS THIS IT?

Am I completely happy? What is my happiness? What does it mean? What is my purpose on this earth? This relates to all aspects of my life – work, family, body, mind and spirit.

Feeling better on the outside. Now to work on the inside. It is a start anyway.

I've come to realise that this is the first of many 28 days. It doesn't end after next week; it has only just begun. That can be considered exciting or scary; maybe a little bit of both.

CRAVING – it gets to a point, like today and yesterday that I just crave chocolate, something sweet, ice cream or just something.

So frustrating to think 'that is not the answer'.

I'm still working out what 'the answer' is. I'm concerned about my diet, am I losing enough, will it eventually move, shift, leave my body and be gone forever? Am I eating the right thing, am I eating enough, too much? Trial and error I suppose. Understanding your body and how it reacts to what you feed it. Getting the right balance and sticking to it.

Am I putting unrealistic expectations on myself and what I can achieve in 28 days – do I need to wait and see what happens in 28 days and beyond? Maybe.

I am feeling fantastic though. High energy, even tempered, relaxed working through the millions of thoughts running through my mind, many questions of myself, my determination, how long I can continue, will it work, will I one day be happy with the results?

I am a little disappointed at how long it is taking me. But what did I expect, bloody miracles?

At the end of the day – it is all about the jeans – still not there yet.

But the upside, I can feel myself getting stronger – marginally.

Still no alcohol – but now no desire.

Will that happen for the rest of my vices?

Let's hope so.

For me now, it's got to be 28 DAYS AND BEYOND.

Time to rest. Up at 6am for boxing training.

Wednesday, 1st September 2004

Perfectionism and patience.

Four kilos – that's it! All this hard work, sweat, tears, pressure, for four bloody kilos. What a disappointment that is, I don't know what I had in mind, but somehow I thought it was going to be more than that.

I am shattered.

What did I do wrong? It must be something? Did I not run hard enough? Did I not sweat enough? Did I eat the wrong things? Maybe I believed I could do better – but what is better? What did I expect after 28 days? Why am I so disappointed – I've got 20 kilos to lose for God's sake. Why did I, in my crazy world, think that I could lose all of it in 28 days – did I think I was suddenly going to look like all those girls in the gym that I envy so much? Yeah, maybe there was a glimmer of hope that in 28 days I would actually look at myself and feel something other than detest, maybe that I would see something other than my flaws, my fat, my ugliness, maybe I just thought that I was going to find the inner strength that has somehow escaped me recently.

I've still got a long way to go. A lifetime in fact. In this body.

So I keep running. Physically and psychologically – I wish I could run away from my inner demons. They seem to be getting worse. Why did I decide to undertake this challenge? Some days I wish I didn't confront these inner thoughts. Other days I'm glad I'm doing it now. I hope that I am gaining the knowledge to deal with whatever presents itself in my future. One day I will look back on this and laugh. I hope so anyway. I know I'm having a bad day. But it is all part of it, isn't it? Four kilos. Hopefully tomorrow those four kilos represent a lot more than they seem to right now. Fingers crossed.

Monday, 6th September 2004

It is funny how people perceive you:

Some see you as a strong independent woman.

Some as an emotional mess.

Some as a hard worker.

Some as a complainer.

Some as a liability.

Some as an asset.

Some as a comic.

Some as a threat.

Some as a friend.

But at the end of the day, I am probably all those things to different people at different times and circumstances throughout my life. As we all are.

What is it that I am today?

I'm so sick of feeling like this all the time. Why do I feel so awful all the time?

A time of uncertainty, questioning, understanding or not understanding what is happening around me, inside me.

Has it in fact, got anything to do with exercising?

I don't think so. Exercising makes me feel so great, so alive, the blood pumps through my veins, my body aches, but in the way I want it to. It has some purpose; for that fleeting moment it has me smiling. A feeling of accomplishment, a sense of achievement. A test of will – that I actually do something that I may not want to, but deem necessary to survive in this world.

Learning to see things differently without all the same tired associations. Maybe that is how I need to look at myself, my body. All aspects of my life. Craig keeps telling me my body is not the problem, maybe it's my tragic self-esteem and thinking – perhaps he's right. I still hate my arse though.

How can we do 'not much' but be busy all the time doing 'stuff?'

Who is it I am – now? This is what I want to explore over the next phase. I want to understand the person inside. Let my mouth speak from my heart. Let me communicate. How and why I'm feeling. Be open and honest. Find my spirit; recapture the true being that is my make up. Laugh, cry, be sad, be happy, be scared, BE BE BE the real me, whoever that person is. It starts here and now. It will be a new adventure. It should end well. I think. It is exciting. First I must sleep. Tomorrow I write. Later I travel. RELAX. I will find it one day. True and complete happiness.

Poor Craig. I think I am a handful for him at times, then again, he's probably used to it. He always tells me that I make it harder than it needs to be and that I have a gift for focusing on the negative. I know he's right ... hate that. It's a journey and I'm on my way. For the first time, I actually feel like I'll make it.

Craig Harper says:

Isn't it interesting to read a person's honest, innermost thoughts as they struggle to get in shape and change their reality? Reading Marlo's diary, you would think she was a morbidly obese ogre. The truth is she is an attractive girl, who could probably lose eight to 10 kilos MAXIMUM (not 20!). I spoke to her this morning (two weeks after the conclusion of her diary entries) and she seems a lot more optimistic and a lot less self-defeating. She has lost another two kilos (six in total) and told me she is finally 'getting it'. Sometimes it takes a while ... go Marlo.

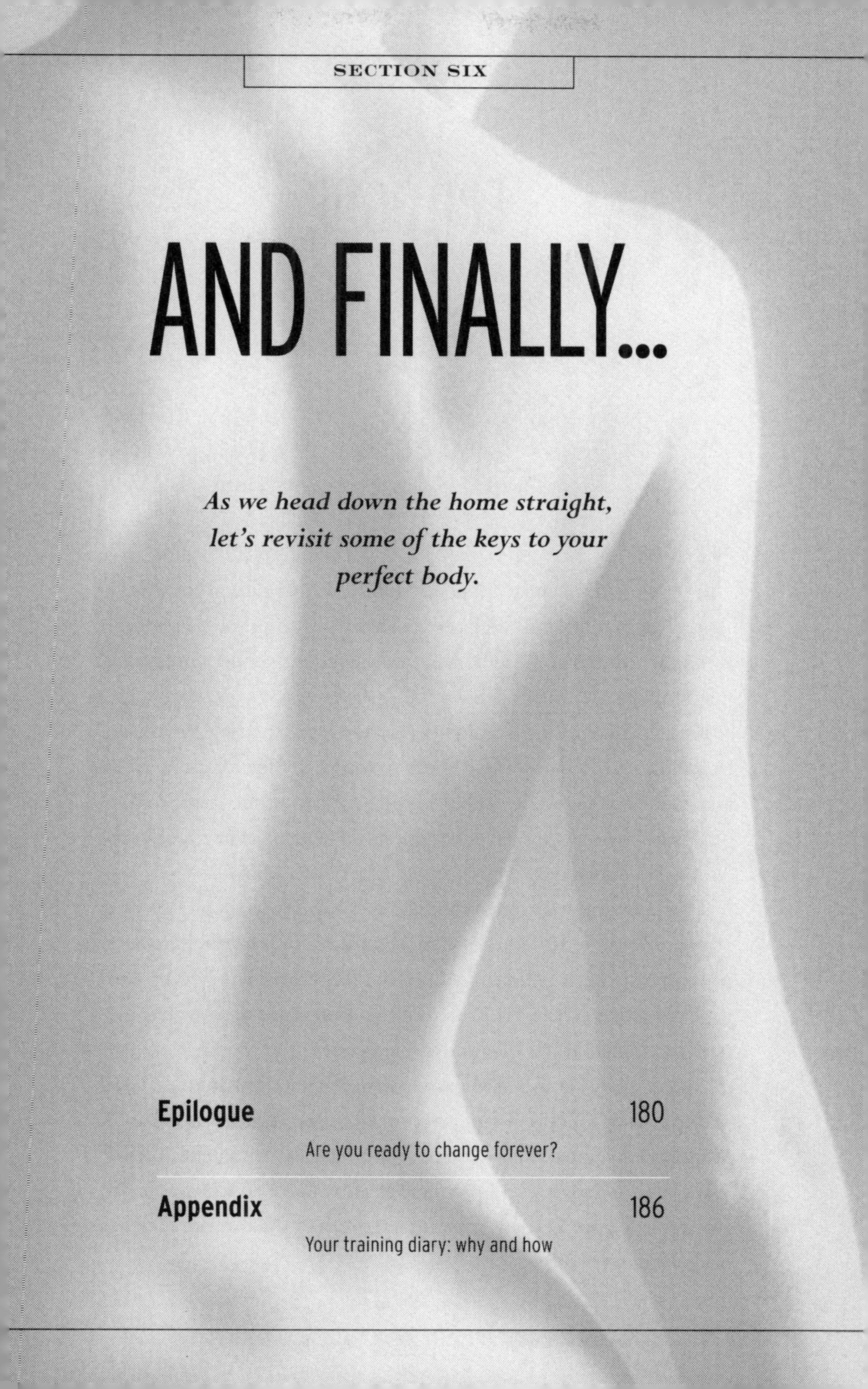

SECTION SIX

AND FINALLY...

As we head down the home straight, let's revisit some of the keys to your perfect body.

Epilogue 180

Are you ready to change forever?

Appendix 186

Your training diary: why and how

EPILOGUE

Are you ready to change forever?

Until recently, I had absolutely no inclination to write a book. I still don't consider myself to be an author but rather a guy who has a message that some people might need to hear.

As an educator and a trainer I reached a point where I realised that while it is apparent that there exists an abundance of exercise and diet information available to the general public, it is also glaringly obvious that despite this glut of information, the average Australian continues to get slightly fatter each year.

This brought me to the realisation that maybe the solution was not about providing more and more information on subjects which have already been written about too many times, but maybe it was time someone wrote a book about the dieter and the exerciser (you), rather that the diet and the exercise.

Maybe the issue is not about carbohydrate and protein ratios or some new super weight loss product. Perhaps it is about us as individuals; how we see our bodies, how we think about food and exercise and how we psychologically approach the process of getting in shape. Perhaps creating forever results is more about our brain than our biceps.

I know it is.

As I have said before, if it was only about accessing information we would all be in great shape because we all have access to at least basic information on exercise and diet if we want it. Most people have more than enough knowledge, skills, time and intelligence to create a fitter, leaner and healthier body yet many are consistently out of shape, consistently looking for the easy option and consistently putting their health at risk. We often look for answers in all the wrong places when sometimes all we really need to do is take a look in the mirror. Ironic isn't it?

If all we did was walk or jog every day and consistently eat less we would be a much leaner and healthier nation. But we continue to look for some miracle, quick-fix solution.

We continue to make it more complex and difficult than it needs to be.

When I was in my late teens I started reading everything about exercise and nutrition that I could get my hands on; books, magazines, journals and research reports; some of them credible, some of them not so credible. I spent thousands of hours reading everything from trashy muscle-mags to research articles which were often beyond my level of understanding or comprehension. In a way, I guess I was hoping to discover the secret which was going to give me the incredible physique I dreamt of as a kid. I read a lot and I learnt a lot. Unfortunately (or fortunately, depends how you look at it), one day I woke up when I was in my early 30s, I owned three gyms, was a respected and well-known personal trainer and I was fat.

I wasn't just carrying a few extra pounds. I was really fat; nearly 40 kilograms heavier than I am now.

I had the knowledge, I had the resources and I certainly had a reason to be in shape (being a fat personal trainer is not a good career move) but there I was; a block of flats in a tracksuit.

One day I was sitting thinking about the whole me thing and I had a 'moment.' It was as though a switch was turned on in my head and I realised more than ever before that I was the problem and the solution. I had been looking for answers in the wrong place. It wasn't about educating myself more (although education is great), it wasn't about going to another workshop or discovering some new supplement. It was about me making some life-changing decisions and committing myself to change my thinking, my attitudes, my beliefs and my body no matter what.

Forever.

I know that some of what I have written may not be welcomed or embraced by everyone and I also know that for many people this book will be quite confrontational.

If you have found parts of the book challenging then that is a good thing; I would prefer that you were confronted and actually moved to take action than you were entertained and amused but still sadly out of shape in six months.

Hopefully you were confronted and amused! I know that if you have made it this far then you have connected with some of the ideas, thoughts and stories within these pages.

The good news is that right now you have the potential to achieve beyond your wildest dreams. This is not a motivational spiel on my behalf; this is a fact. Whether or not you will achieve is up to you.

Most of us base our expectations for the future on what we have or have not achieved to this point in our lives. What you have achieved up to now is usually no indication of your potential or what you could be or do in the future.

Most of us spend most of our lives underachieving when we don't need to. Make sure you don't.

I have faith in you and I have not even met you!

IN SUMMARY

Here is my summary for you:

1. Make some genuine life decisions and follow through – by not making a decision you are making a decision.

2. Professional help can make a big difference, but common sense is a good start.

3. Set goals, create plans and expect good things.

4. It is not about knowing, it's about doing.

5. Different things work for different people.

6. Start gradually, build up gently.

7. Finish what you start – don't be forever starting a new program.

8. Stop looking for the easy way – look for the most effective way.

9. Think big picture – in shape forever, not for a wedding.

10. Approach everything with a good attitude – don't make it harder than it needs to be.

11. Accept complete responsibility for where you are, what you do and don't achieve.

>>

IN SUMMARY

12. Don't base your expectations for the future on your past.

13. Don't always avoid discomfort – it is part of growth and sometimes we need it.

14. Be consistent – most people are erratic with their eating and their exercise.

15. Diarise everything.

16. Make getting in shape a logical, rational process; not an emotional one.

17. Don't expect everyone to be happy for you as you begin to achieve.

18. Enjoy the support of others but don't be dependent on anyone – it is about personal empowerment.

19. Have fun – laugh at yourself – don't be a pain to be around.

20. Don't do it for someone else, do it for you.

21. A lower bodyfat percentage will not fix a dysfunctional relationship.

>>

IN SUMMARY

22. Lots of people are wealthy in some ways and destitute in others. You only have one body so look after it.

23. Sometimes what we need to hear is not what we want to hear.

24. Insanity is doing the same thing over and over and expecting a different outcome.

25. Bodies are very adaptable and can change quickly; minds take a little longer.

26. Fat kids don't have to become fat adults. Fat adults don't have to stay fat.

27. Learn to listen to your body – it knows what you need.

28. We all create our own reality.

29. Motivation comes and goes – stay focused anyway.

30. For many people, the right time never comes. Don't be one of those people.

31. It is not about time – it is about you.

32. Sometimes it is not fun or exciting or easy – but it is all worth it!

APPENDIX

Your training diary: why and how.

For all the reasons I've outlined previously (commitment, organisation, accountability etc.) keeping a diary can be a valuable part of the process. It is my experience that people who go to the trouble of filling out a diary each day stay motivated and focused for longer, and are much more likely to achieve their goals. Keeping a diary is not about becoming obsessed (as some people tell me), it's about becoming more responsible, more aware, more disciplined and more productive. If you have decided to keep a diary here are some guidelines:

- Anything which will impact on the end result (how you look, feel and function) should be in the diary; this includes everything that goes into your mouth: food, coffee, tea, water, alcohol – everything!
- Exercise Information should be detailed: sets, reps, weight, distances, intensity level, duration – this way you can gauge progress over time.
- Write in times: times of meals, when you get up, when you go to bed.
- Do your best to maintain a diary for at least six months – even when you're bored!
- Include things like supplements, energy levels, moods and general comments (any relevant information).

- Be vigilant: don't miss days and do you best to record your behaviour through the day (as you go) rather than at the end of the day.
- Be completely honest and accurate with the diary.

By keeping a diary over time you will begin to discover what works best for your body. Remember, different bodies need different approaches, so it is imperative that we learn what works best for us (specifically) in terms of food, exercise, supplements, recovery and lifestyle. As I write this I have people ranging from eight year old school children to 50 year old doctors who are filling out their 'health' diaries every day – all achieving great results.

So, start writing!

Example of a food and training diary entry.

harper's
personal training

DATE: 30/9/04

WEIGHTS

Exercise	Sets & Reps					
	1	2	3	4	5	6
BENCH PRESS:	15/100,	12/130,	10/160,	8/200		
LAT PULLS	15/100,	12/120,	10/140,	8/160		
SHOULDER PRESS (MACHINE)	15/80,	12/120,	8/160			
TRICEP PUSHDOWNS:	15/60,	12/70,	10/80			
BB CURLS:	15/50,	12/60,	10/70			
ABS:	20	20	20			

Body Parts Trained: Upper.

CARDIO

Exercise	Amount
WALK	30 MINS - (easy)
BIKE	15 " - (moderate)

FOOD & TRAINING DIARY

FOOD			
l	Time	Qty	Description
	6.45	3	Pcs. Rye toast & sugar-free jam
	9.15	1	lf yoghurt
		1	Apple.
	12.00	1	chicken, salad pita wrap
	2.30	1	protein drink
	6.00	1	Beef, veggie stirfry & Basmati rice
	7.30	1	small fruit salad.
* 3 Coffees today.			

er(Glasses	1	2	3	4	5	6	7	8	9	10	11	12	13	14	15
	X	X	X	X	X	X	X								

plements:						
e to sleep last nt:	11.30	Mood:	Exc.	Good X	Fair	Poor
e awake today:	6.15	Energy:	Exc. X	High	Fair	Low
ents:						

My ankle is still a little sore, getting better slowly.

ABOUT THE AUTHOR

Craig Harper is one of Australia's leading presenters and motivators in the areas of health, fitness and lifestyle management. A qualified exercise scientist, he has worked as a personal trainer, corporate consultant, personal development speaker, university lecturer, AFL strength coach, health and fitness writer, radio presenter and is a successful business owner.

In the past 20 years he has worked with thousands of people, ranging from frustrated dieters through to world champion athletes, all hoping to achieve roughly the same thing; physical change.

Establishing one of Australia's first personal training centres in 1991, Craig is considered by many to be something of a pioneer in the fitness scene. Since the early 1990s, he and his staff have completed approximately 250,000 personal training sessions, worked with numerous companies, organisations and teams and have helped change many lives, attitudes and bodies along the way.

Craig lives in Melbourne, Australia and owns and operates one of the nation's largest personal training facilities, a 10,000 square-foot centre in Brighton.

Over the last decade Craig has written for various newspapers and magazines, the most notable the *Herald Sun* where he was a regular contributor for three years. Craig has appeared on *Today Tonight* and *A Current Affair* and can be heard weekly on Melbourne radio station SEN.

Craig works on a daily basis with individuals and organisations, educating and inspiring them to create their optimum lifestyle and body, and specialises in helping people deal with old issues in new ways.

He has immense empathy for, and understanding of, those who constantly struggle with the issues of obesity, motivation and self-esteem, having been an obese child and teenager. Weighing 90 kilograms as a 14-year-old has given him a unique perspective and insight into dealing with the issues of health, weight loss and creating change.

ACKNOWLEDGEMENTS

The slightly naïve personal trainer from the gym on the highway had no idea about what was involved in producing a book. Should only take a few weeks on the lap-top, bit of tidying up, a few spell checks, a couple of proof reads, chuck in a photo or two, get some bloke who knows a bit about publishing and marketing and we're done. Five or six weeks tops. Just squeeze it in between the other commitments.

How hard could it be?

Plenty.

A year and fifty gazillion man-hours later, I now realise how little I know about so many things and how many smart and talented people are required to take a book from an idea in my head to a finished product.

In no particular order, a big thanks to:

- The team at GSP – you're ace.
- Paul Marcolin – thanks for believing in me and the book.
- Marky Mark Lang and the team at Moski.
- My trusty team of proof readers – Julie Warren, Kim Williamson, Renea Stoupas, Patrick Bonello, Libbi Herries and Jan 'check out me guns' Frazer.
- Russell Rzechta – thanks for your constant support.
- Pauline Mary Grosman – thanks for providing me with so much material!
- Ailsa Piper – thanks for telling me what I need to hear, not necessarily what I want to hear.
- Vin Harris – just cause you'll love your name in a book!
- Ron and Mary – love you wacky kids, thanks for my first barbell.
- Marie Rechner – thanks for bringing order into my chaotic life and business.
- Jobbas – shirt off!
- The Harper's trainers – who teach me new things every day.
- All the people who told me that there was no market for personal training or fitness consulting in Australia – thanks for the motivation.
- My spiritual support crew – Big Bucky, Little Bucky, Phill, Gras.
- The Big Guy who gave me the gifts and the talent to do what I do.